10-22-06

David,

I have found the book "dynamic" in my efforts at developing Boards — Hope you do as well.

John Manning

Developing
Dynamic Boards

A Proactive Approach to Building
Nonprofit Boards of Directors

Developing Dynamic Boards

A Proactive Approach to Building
Nonprofit Boards of Directors

JAMES M. HARDY, PH.D.

F P ESSEX PRESS
Erwin, Tennessee

Also by James M. Hardy
   Focus on the Family
   Using Sensitivity Training and the Laboratory Method
      (with R. L. Batchelder)
   Corporate Planning for Nonprofit Organizations
   Managing Individual Development
   Managing for Impact in Nonprofit Organizations

Library of Congress catalog card number: 89–082351

To communicate with James M. (Bo) Hardy, or for more information about James M. Hardy Associates' consultation and training services, contact:
   James M. Hardy Associates
   800 Pippin Hollow Road
   Erwin, Tennessee 37650
   (423) 743-7685, PH & FAX

Printed and bound in United States of America.

ISBN: 0–930381–02–5

Reprinted 1994

To

CLYDE McMAHON

My first board chairman—leader, teacher and friend

For your magnificient contributions
in the lives of people and in society.

Contents

Part Three   Appendix and Bibliography

Exhibits

Chapter 2

Chapter 3

Chapter 4

Chapter 5

Chapter 6

Chapter 7

Chapter 8

Chapter 9

Chapter 11

Preface

This book is about developing boards of directors—those sometimes maligned but more often forgotten and neglected policy groups—which are assumedly at the helm of nonprofit organizations in our society. The evidence indicates that, in the main, boards need help in fulfilling their functions of governance, stewardship and support. The purpose of this book is to provide board chairs and chief executives the understanding, tools and techniques that can improve the functioning of boards of directors. Certainly this work is not the final or complete word in board development. Hopefully, however, it will be a helpful beginning.

This book's approach is quite different from the more traditional and time honored approaches found in much of the literature on boards. Some might even call it radical. Essentially, the book's basic thesis is that boards of directors can and, indeed, must be developed. It rejects the assumption that boards are "givens" to board chairs and to chief executives; that is, that boards cannot be changed. On the contrary, this book is based on the proposition that board chairs and chief executives are responsible for developing boards of directors—building them, if you will—into dynamic, fully functioning and very human mechanisms that provide organizational direction and policy undergirding.

Although I have stated and will continue to state in the text that the responsibility for giving leadership to board development rests with the board chair and the chief executive, I do recommend that a board development committee be appointed. I recognize that the one thing which most nonprofits need least is another committee. However, the job of board development is on-going and so crucial that it merits the detailed oversight of a standing committee. The board development committee replaces the nominating committee, but as the reader will soon see, the functions of a board development committee go far beyond, but include the functions of a typical nominating committee.

In writing this book, I found myself constantly encountering two concerns, neither of which I feel are completely resolved. Consequently, I solicit your understanding and assistance on both. My *first concern* is the tendency when writing about systems, approaches, methods and the like, for the writing to be de-humanizing. I hope the reader will join me in constantly reminding ourselves that board development is a very human endeavor—that it deals with real people who have real feelings and needs and who have very important jobs to do. Although the descriptions of some techniques and systems in this book may sound very mechanistic and de-humanizing, that is never the intent. I need each reader's assistance in making my intent real. My *second concern* is that some of the tools, techniques and processes described in this book appear to be very complex due to the explanations and descriptions which I have provided. I'm frankly very ambivalent about how much detail to include. I want the reader to have enough detail to support utilization, but not so much as to be inundated or perhaps even immobilized. In my efforts to strike this delicate balance, I may have caused some tools and techniques to appear much more complex in the written word than they actually are when put into practice. I therefore earnestly request the reader's understanding and hope that you will get beyond the words and into the doing. If you can do this, I think you will find, as Mark Twain said about Wagner's music, "It's not as bad as it sounds."

This book, like two of my previous efforts, is designed to be used, not just read. I suggest that you consider reading Part One (first three chapters) to get an overview of the nonprofit sector and an understanding of boards and clarification of the volunteer-staff relationship. You may then want to have the entire board or the board development committee use the "Board Development Assessment" (Appendix A), complete the "Assessment Response Grid" (Appendix B) and score it with the "Tabulation Sheet" (Appendix C). This will clearly indicate the dimensions of board development that are of greatest need to your organization. The board development committee can then use the "Board Development Key" (Appendix D) to construct a comprehensive board development program. This process will allow you to obtain maximum use from Part Two (Components of Board Development) of this book based on the areas of greatest need of your organization.

At many places in the book I have suggested optional tools, techniques and processes. I encourage you to either select from the options presented or to use them for developing approaches that better suit your circumstances. Please feel free to reproduce instruments, handouts or designs in this book for use in your organization or to adapt any of the material to make it more useful to you and your organization. However, I must insert one restriction—please *do not* reproduce any material from this book either for sale or distribution outside of your organization.

In every book that I have written, I am always indebted to many individuals and groups for their assistance. This seems particularly true for this book. First and foremost are the board members, board chairs and chief executives of literally hundreds of nonprofit organizations with whom I've worked. Working with boards of all shapes and sizes and in a variety of organizations has been a rare privilege for me and an unusual learning opportunity. I'm greatly indebted to each of these boards for the many things that they have taught me and for the testing and feedback which they have provided on the concepts, processes, tools and techniques contained in this book. Through testing and refinement they have validated the suggestions and ideas in this book. This could not have been accomplished without them. My gratitude to each of them is only exceeded by my respect for the caring contributions that they are making to our society.

I am also indebted to many colleagues in the behavioral and management sciences for their prior research and writings. I have drawn liberally from many previous works and I've attempted to acknowledge these contributions to my thinking and to this book in the "Notes" at the end of each chapter. My appreciation goes to each of those whose creative contributions have been both helpful and inspiring to me.

I'm indebted to several colleagues for their critical reviews and feedback on the original manuscript of this book. I'm especially appreciative of the gentle but definitive editorial assistance of Carol Crawford.

Finally, and as always, I'm indebted to my wife, Bettye. Simply stated, this book would never have seen the light of day without her insights and multiple contributions—all of which defy description. She is absolutely amazing; not only in what she accomplishes with seemingly gracious ease and competence, but also with what she inspires in all of those around her. For me, her astounding productivity, caring presence, sensitive involvements and constant humor have combined to make the writing of this book a true labor of love.

James M. Hardy

Part One

Overview of the Voluntary Sector and Board Functioning

chapter 1.

Introduction to Board Development

Context: The Voluntary Sector

Each reader of this book is probably familiar, some intimately so, with the voluntary sector of society. Variously labeled the nonprofit sector, the third sector (business and government being the other two) or more recently the independent sector—most of us are frequently touched, and many deeply affected, by voluntary organizations. Perhaps, however, like the majority of Americans, we tend to take the voluntary sector for granted. To off-set this tendency and to provide a context for our thinking, let's remind ourselves of three characteristics of this major sector of our society.

First, the voluntary sector is a mixed bag. It encompasses an extraordinary array of organizations—religious groups, museums, libraries, schools and colleges, symphony orchestras, health care organizations, community action and advocacy groups, neighborhood groups and countless other voluntary organizations such as Girl Scouts

3

and Boy Scouts, YM and YWCA's, Girls Clubs and Boys Clubs, the Salvation Army, United Ways, Red Cross, Urban League, Volunteers of America, Alcoholics Anonymous, to name just a few. Some are huge with multimillion dollar budgets and others get by with a part-time clerk or an unpaid secretary. Some are staffed by well trained and sophisticated professionals, others by volunteers with great dedication. Some are funded by contributions and federated support, others primarily by program and membership fees, and still others are supported entirely or in part by tax dollars. As stated by John W. Gardner, "In its diversity and strength the voluntary sector is uniquely American— not in the fact of its existence, because it exists elsewhere, but in its extraordinary richness and variety."[1] There are, however, common characteristics of organizations that make up this diverse sector: they are private, they are devoted to serving the general welfare, and they are governed by a board of directors who are volunteers.

Second, the voluntary sector is big and still growing. Apparently it is difficult to determine precisely the size of the sector. Recent research indicates that in two decades the number of nonprofits has tripled, climbing from 309,000 in 1967, to just under one million currently.[2] Others estimate the current number of nonprofits from 1.2 million to six million.[3] The combined gross receipts of nonprofits approximate $275 billion a year or about seven percent of the gross national product. There are about seven million paid employees in the nonprofit sector representing 7.07 percent of the nation's nonagricultural workforce. The combined value of volunteer time given to organizations in the sector is estimated at $70 billion to $150 billion.[4,5,6] Regardless of the figures used, it is clear that the voluntary sector is huge.

Third, the voluntary sector is important to the American way of life. Millions of Americans participate in the programs, services and activities of the sector and derive direct benefits. In addition to having a direct and positive effect on the vast majority of Americans, the voluntary sector has, as pointed out by John D. Rockefeller III, been the seedbed for organized efforts to deal with social problems. All

4

important contemporary movements have sprung from the voluntary sector—civil rights, workers' rights, consumerism, the environment and many others.

Perspective: Voluntary Organizations

Where did it begin—this movement to be of service to others? One must search far back in the history of Western Civilization for the origins of voluntary effort. Indeed, from the very beginning of human existence as modern sociology and anthropology have evidenced, men and women have striven to share with as well as to destroy their fellows. Starting with the family, the kin and extending to the tribe and the early communities, men and women had to cooperate and care for one another just to survive in the face of hostile environments.

History has recorded numberless instances of individual and group effort to promote the common good. These efforts have frequently been accomplished at great sacrifice and risk. Most historians agree that the impulse for these acts is found in the Judeo-Christian ethos of love, justice and mercy. Most volunteers and voluntary organizations in our society today can trace their lineage and inspiration to these devoted efforts.

Although people have banded together since the beginning of time for many reasons, modern associational forms of voluntary effort were stimulated by the Reformation, defined by the urbanization of society during the Industrial Revolution, and experienced their greatest expansion during the twentieth century. These voluntary organizations were formed to fulfill an incredible variety of purposes, ranging from the individual needs of members to services to individuals and to communities.[7] The inspiration down through the ages for countless legions to give of themselves in service to others seems clear—the great

5

idea of one common humanity and of the basic dignity and worth of all persons without exception.[8]

It is important to note that all associational forms of voluntary effort were founded, developed and initially operated by volunteers. In these early organizations the entire responsibility for conducting the programs and affairs of the organization was in the hands of volunteers. As organizations grew, volunteers found they could no longer handle all the work themselves and staff were employed by many of these organizations to take over some of the responsibilities formerly exercised completely by volunteers.

Since the employment of staff by voluntary organizations, there have been forces with varying degrees of intensity that have mitigated against the full utilization of volunteers as members of boards and committees. Among the most recent are:

● **Accelerated Rate of Change**—This has, in the view of some, necessitated speeding up decision making—shortcutting the processes in order to shorten the time lag in transforming policies and decisions into practice and program.

● **Concepts of Management**—In some cases influential board members have grown inpatient with what they perceive as staff's preoccupation in giving too much time in working with boards and committees and in utilizing involvement processes. In other cases employed staff have assumed a stronger initiating role in decision making and have relied less on boards and committees for certain decisions.

● **Time Demands on Volunteers**—The accelerated pace of American living combined with increasing time demands by employers and growing competition for leadership among voluntary organizations has forced many qualified people to restrict their voluntary activities. For some, this has resulted in extreme reliance on staff to fulfill some board responsibilities.

● **Increase of Women in Workforce**—This development has substantially reduced the number of women available for long-term volunteer board and committee activity.[9]

● **Increased Complexity in Program and Operation**—Nonprofits have become increasingly involved in a variety of sophisticated program activities and complex facility and financial operations. The sheer growth of many nonprofits has also substantially increased the complexity of operations. Many of these endeavors require highly skilled, well-trained technicians and the application of relatively new methods and approaches. In some cases this has led to either a complete reliance on staff or the assumption of new responsibilities by staff and resulted in a lessening of the volunteer policy-making role.

In spite of the countervailing forces at work, it has been known for some time that the most vital and healthy nonprofits are those that have strengthened rather than constricted the volunteer role. Indeed, in reporting the results of their intensive research into the health of voluntary organizations, Lippincott and Aannestad stated in the *Harvard Business Review*, "The most important element in agency structure is the membership and activity of its board of directors. No other aspect of a voluntary agency is a more certain indicator to the state of its health or more crucial to that health."[10] Today when nonprofits are feeling close scrutiny—by the press, the legal profession, taxing agencies and the general public—there is an even greater need for nonprofit board and committee members capable of intelligent, informed inquiry that leads to enlightened and significant action for the common good.

Board Development

As important as boards of directors are, there is mounting evidence that the governing boards of many nonprofits govern poorly or not at all. Based on his recent research, John Nason states:

7

". . . the governing boards of a majority of nonprofits govern badly, if at all. In many instances the members provide window dressing, an aura of responsibility. Their presence usually reflects a certain amount of good will, though often good will toward the friend who asked them to join as much as toward the organization itself. In too many situations they are passive rather than active, prepared to go along without rocking the boat. In others they are too involved in management matters, often a carry-over from an earlier day when there was no fulltime staff."[11]

Kenneth N. Dayton goes even further, stating:

"It has long been my conviction that too many (nonprofit) institutions have underemphasized the importance of good management and good governance. Somehow, being nonprofit has become an excuse for being nonprofessional."[12]

I suspect that most observers of the voluntary sector and the majority of practitioners in the sector would agree that nonprofit boards need to be further developed. There would be considerable divergence, however, on what is meant by board development and, indeed, what is needed. My experience indicates that most practitioners think of board development as simply "getting more people with money and influence on the board" or "getting more power people on the board." That's a very limiting and short-term point of view. Obtaining people of money, influence and power may or may not be important for any agency's board. Regardless, it falls far short of comprehensive board development. In my judgment, board development is an on-going process of building and developing an agency board of directors that will preserve and enhance the character, growth and influence of the agency and maximize the agency's contribution in the lives of people and in the community it serves.

Board development has many parts. A dozen of the key components are:

8

Assessment of Board Members—Assessing the board in relationship to eight factors for board effectiveness (Chapter 4). This is the starting point of board development and involves the use of a systematic process for an agency to assess where its board is in relationship to each factor, what it needs to move the agency ahead and the strategies it will use for building the desired board.

Identification of Board Members—Identifying the individual characteristics and persons who are needed and can contribute to actualizing the agency's desired future. These desired characteristics are derived from the previously noted assessment of board members.

Rotation—Moving board members systematically to provide a constant flow of new thinking into the agency's governance structure. This also involves ridding the board of "dead wood."

Retention—Developing methods for retaining helpful people and utilizing their resources in ways other than through membership on boards.

Cultivation—Providing opportunities for prospective board members to be exposed to the agency and its work prior to board membership. This also involves keeping people informed of the work of the agency and involving them in short-term tasks and activities.

Recruitment—Developing and implementing the strategies for getting needed board members.

Organization and Effective Functioning—Giving creative attention, as needed, to team development and conducting productive and satisfying meetings in addition to the more mechanical but very important elements of board functioning, such as size, frequency of meetings and committee structure.

Orientation—Conducting an annual orientation for new board members regarding the agency and the board's role, functions and relationships.

9

Use of Members' Resources—Ensuring the participation and involvement of all board members and the fullest possible utilization of each member's resources.

Training and Education—Providing on-going training and educational opportunities that go beyond orientation and that facilitate effective functioning for all board members.

Evaluation—Providing systematic methods and opportunities for self-evaluation of board functioning and productivity with feedback mechanisms and the development and implementation of improvement actions.

Recognition—Giving continuous attention to multiple ways of providing deserved recognition of volunteer services.

Each reader can add significantly to these components of board development and I hope you will. In total, the components provide a systematic approach for supporting and assisting an agency's board of directors in effectively carrying out its role, functions and relationships as delineated in the next chapter.

NOTES: *Chapter 1*

1. Gardner, John W. "The Independent Sector." *America's Voluntary Spirit.* Brian O'Connell. The Foundation Center, 1983, p. IX.

2. Weisbrod, Burton A. *The Nonprofit Economy.* Harvard University Press, 1989.

3. *Formal Education of Nonprofit Organization Leaders/Managers.* Independent Sector, 1988, p. 4.

4. Barbeito, Carol L. *Doing Good Can Mean Doing Well.* Technical Assistance Center, 1985, p. 2.

5. Rudney, Gabriel. "The Scope and Dimension of Nonprofit Activity." *The Nonprofit Sector* edited by Walter W. Powell. Yale University Press, 1987, pp. 56–57.

6. Drucker, Peter F. "What Business Can Learn From Nonprofits." *Harvard Business Review*, July-August, 1989, p. 88.

7. Manser, Gordon and Rosemary Higgins Cass. *Voluntarism at The Crossroads*. Family Service Association of America, 1976, pp. 19–36.

8. Titmuss, Richard M. *The Gift Relationship: From Human Blood to Social Policy*. Pantheon Books, 1971.

9. Fram, Eugene H. "Nonprofit Boards: They're Going Corporate." *Board Leadership and Governance*. The Society for Nonprofit Organizations, 1989, p. 25.

10. Lippincott, E., E. Aannestad. "Management of Voluntary Welfare Agencies." *Harvard Business Review*, Vol. 46, No. 6, 1964, p. 88.

11. Nason, John W. *An Inquiry Into Current Program Toward Strengthening The Performance of Board Members of Nonprofit Organizations*. Association of Governing Boards of Universities and Colleges, 1984, p. 3.

12. Dayton, Kenneth N. *Governance Is Governance*. Independent Sector, 1987, p. 1.

chapter 2.

Role, Functions and Responsibilities of the Board of Directors

Role of the Board

The board of directors of a voluntary organization is vested with the responsibility for the governance and direction of the organization. Some writers state that the role of the board is to manage the organization. I find this very misleading since management implies the conduct of day-to-day affairs which should be the responsibility of employed staff. For me, *governance* is a much more appropriate word for describing the role of the board.[1]

Most nonprofit organizations are incorporated under the laws of the state in which they operate. The articles of incorporation or the organization's nonprofit charter define the role, functions and duties of the board.

In general, however, the role of the board of directors may be described as follows:

● **Planning and Policy Decisions**—Setting the agency's direction (its mission, goals and objectives); establishing policies to guide the operation of the agency; hiring the chief executive officer (chief employed staff person).

● **Financial Development**—Responsibility for funding the planning and policy decisions and for ensuring that the agency is adequately financed.

● **Monitoring and Sanction**—Monitoring the implementation of planning and policy decisions to ensure the achievement of goals and objectives; providing sanction, enthusiastic endorsement and approval of the agency to the community, based on real achievements and contributions to community betterment.

In carrying out these three key elements of its role, the board is accountable to the community and to the agency's funding sources. In the first instance the accountability pertains primarily to the quality and relevance of programs and services rendered to clients, constituents or members. In fulfilling its accountability to the funding sources, the agency accounts for monies spent by budgetary techniques.[2]

As the ultimate planning and policy-making body of the agency, a responsible board of directors will manage not to get involved in too much detail. Its emphasis will be on goals, objectives, strategies and policies. It will never duplicate what the chief executive officer has been employed to do, but rather it will hold the CEO accountable for implementation of planning and policy decisions. It will establish other volunteer groups (committees, councils and task forces) and look to these groups for operational planning, policy recommendations and two-way communications between itself and the membership/constituency at large.

Functions of the Board

The specific major functions of the board of directors are to:

● **Formulate and approve long range goals and objectives**

Some theorists state that the board should approve the long range goals based on the recommendation of the CEO. Many board members from business and industry are proponents of this idea where it is common practice. I think such a view is short-sighted and inadequate. In my opinion, boards must be intimately involved in *formulating* long range goals in addition to finally approving the goals. Furthermore, the board should approve or delegate approval of annual objectives and priorities established to achieve long range goals. Detailed assistance for these functions is provided in the planning literature and will not be restated here.[3]

● **Formulate and adopt policies**

One of the major failures of nonprofit boards is that they get bogged down in operating details instead of governing. It seems that otherwise intelligent individuals and, in many cases, astute business people, often toss aside the principles of good management, and sometimes even common sense, and plunge into administrative minutiae when they become nonprofit board members. Richard Chait and Barbara Taylor have found at least five reasons that may draw boards into chronic involvement with operational details: 1) Trustees may have specialized knowledge; 2) Trustees may have a special interest; 3) Some trustees would rather act than delegate; 4) Trustees tend to manage during an internal transition or crisis; 5) Trustees may manage in periods of external turbulence and crisis.[4]

One of the major ways for a board to stay out of day-to-day operations is to focus its efforts on the board functions of formulating and adopting policy. Many boards, however, are unclear regarding the policy function. In a comprehensive definition, the Public Management Institute in San Francisco states that policy is: 1) A governing principle;

14

2) A framework for carrying out work; 3) A way for the board to delegate authority and still maintain control; 4) A way to develop plans, solve problems and attain objectives; 5) A way to ensure uniformity and consistency of action throughout the organization; 6) A way to specify service priorities; 7) A way to speed up decisions; 8) A definition of what is to be done and where effort is to go—not how to do it; 9) Always written down; 10) Never a final and absolute product.

Obviously there are many levels of policies. The trick is for the board to concentrate its talent and energies on policy levels that have the greatest impact on the agency's future and that are most important. Richard Hodgetts and Max S. Wortman, Jr. have developed an administrative model that identifies six policy levels, ranging from "major policies" concerned with fundamental issues of mission to "rules" that guide everyday conduct.[5] Exhibit I is an adaptation of the model indicating policy decisions for a university, a hospital and a YMCA. For the most part, a board should devote little, if any, energy to lower level policies such as operating procedures and rules. These usually fall too far outside the board's appropriate sphere of concern. But this hierarchy should not be viewed as rigid. Rather it is suggested as a spectrum to assist boards in devoting attention on a selective basis to formulating and adopting high level policy statements.

● **Select, employ, periodically assess and, if necessary, dismiss the chief executive officer**

Certainly one of the most important decisions that a board makes is selecting the agency's chief executive officer. It is not within the purview of this book to replicate the detailed guidance provided in other excellent publications for boards to fulfill this critical function. I particularly like the approach to recruiting and selection of CEO's described by Brian O'Connell, president of Independent Sector, in a booklet that is part of a nonprofit management series.[6] In selecting a new CEO, a strict timetable is very important. A client organization of mine took sixteen months to select an executive director and it was devastating to the organization. Prolonged search operations are unhealthy for the organization's morale and are unnecessarily awkward.

Exhibit I
DECISIONS AT DIFFERENT POLICY LEVELS

POLICY LEVEL	COLLEGES AND UNIVERSITIES	HOSPITALS	YMCA'S
MAJOR	• Offer graduate education • Discontinue church affiliation • Merge with another campus	• Medical school affiliation • HMO affiliation • Care of indigent	• Offer subsidized program in low income areas • Severely curtail adult education • New fitness facility
SECONDARY	• Establish new academic department • Establish educational television station • Admission standards and financial aid criteria	• Medical staff credentialing • Acquisition of big equipment • Incident reporting and quality assurance	• Expansion of service area • Reciprocal membership for all branches • Acquisition of fitness testing equipment
FUNCTIONAL	• Budget approval process • Investment policies • Tuition and fees	• Budget approval process • Investment policies • Fee schedule	• Budget approval process • Investment policies • Membership fees and privileges
MINOR	• Participation in United Way campaign • Selection of consultants • Intercollegiate athletic schedule	• Participation in United Way campaign • Selection of consultants • Employee identification and security	• Participation in United Way campaign • Selection of consultants • Expense policy for volunteers
STANDARD OPERATING PROCEDURES	• Grade appeals • Student discipline • Sabbatical requests	• Emergency evacuation plans • On-call rosters • Emergency room triage	• Staff coverage and supervision • Sunday and holiday schedule • Use of facilities by outside groups
RULES	• Parking • Smoking • Library fines	• Parking • Smoking • Visiting hours	• Parking • Smoking • Guest passes and privileges

O'Connell suggests that at the local level the process should not require more than three months, including time to determine attributes and skills, develop the job description and salary scale, and search for and screen applicants. Others have suggested a process of from four to five and one-half months' duration.[7]

In addition to selecting and employing the chief executive officer, the board should provide support, encouragement, feedback and criticism, as appropriate. Essentially, the board should hold the CEO accountable for implementation of all planning and policy decisions. Accountability, of course, implies the provision of systematic performance review and appraisal of the CEO. It is unfortunate but most nonprofit boards do not provide systematic performance appraisal for CEO's. At best, most nonprofits offer highly informal feedback on a sporadic basis. This is a substantial loss to both the CEO's and the organizations involved.

There are at least three viable mechanisms available to the board for accomplishing the important task of annually appraising the chief executive: 1) The board of directors acting as a committee of the whole can conduct the review and appraisal, particularly if the board is composed of nine or fewer members; 2) The board of directors can provide perceptions and inputs and appoint a small review team to finalize the review and appraisal; 3) A smaller group (e.g., board officers, executive committee or a specially appointed small group of three to five informed persons) can conduct the review and appraisal and report back to the entire board.

If an organization is involved in a comprehensive corporate planning process (with mission, long range goals, short-term objectives and action plans), it is suggested that the CEO's summary report to the board on progress made during the year on achievement of objectives related to long range goals be used as the data base for reviewing and appraising the performance of the chief executive. If these data are available, it is suggested that the "Guide for Annual Review and Appraisal of Chief Executive's Performance" (Exhibit II) be used.[8] The

17

Exhibit II

GUIDE FOR ANNUAL REVIEW AND APPRAISAL
OF CHIEF EXECUTIVE'S PERFORMANCE

CHIEF EXECUTIVE: _____ DATE: _____

BOARD MEMBERS PARTICIPATING IN APPRAISAL: _____

_____

1.	2.	3.	4.	5.
Well Below Standard	*Below Standard*	*On Standard*	*Above Standard*	*Well Above Standard*
(Unsatisfactory)	(Marginal)	(Satisfactory)	(Commendable)	(Outstanding)

I. PERFORMANCE APPRAISAL: ACHIEVEMENT OF OBJECTIVES
(Based on complete review of the organization's achievement of objectives during the past year that are directly related to corporate goals)

    A. High Achievement Areas:

    B. Low Achievement Areas (Improvement needed):

    PERFORMANCE RATING ON ACHIEVEMENT OF ORGANIZATIONAL
    OBJECTIVES: _____

II. PERFORMANCE APPRAISAL: MANAGERIAL EFFECTIVENESS
(Based on discussion and review of relevant data of the past year)

PERFORMANCE AREA	PERFORMANCE RATING	COMMENTS
A. *Affirmative Action* (Performance in achieving the organization's affirmative action goals)		
B. *Board and Committee Development* (Performance of effective executive leadership to board and committees)		
C. *Decision Making* (Performance in decision-making situations, considering alternatives, weighing risks and making firm decisions)		

PERFORMANCE AREA	PERFORMANCE RATING	COMMENTS
D. *Fiscal Management and Control* (Performance in annual budget development, monthly budget monitoring and year-end balanced operations)		
E. *Human Relations Skills* (Performance in communicating effectively; working with, developing and motivating volunteers and staff to attain organizational goals and objectives)		
F. *Initiative* (Performance in moving on situations quickly; taking required actions without being prompted, urged or directed)		
G. *Planning* (Performance in directing the organization's planning process of establishing corporate goals, annual objectives, implementation and feedback)		
H. *Staff Supervision and Development* (Performance of effective executive leadership in selection, training and development of staff)		
I. *Quality and Follow-Through* (Performance in setting high standards of excellence for the organization and keeping the board informed on both achievements and problems)		

PERFORMANCE RATING ON MANAGERIAL EFFECTIVENESS: _____

III. PERFORMANCE SUMMARY

    A. Performance Rating on Achievement of Organizational Objectives. _____

    B. Performance Rating on Managerial Effectiveness .... _____

    C. Overall Rating of Total Performance... _____ *

IV. SUGGESTIONS FOR IMPROVEMENT (Be as specific as possible)

* This rating should be the most important consideration in making a salary adjustment based on merit.

Reprinted with permission from MANAGING FOR IMPACT IN NONPROFIT ORGANIZATIONS by James M. Hardy, Essex Press, 1984.

particular items shown in Part II of the exhibit (Managerial Effectiveness) can, of course, be changed to reflect managerial areas that are deemed most important to the organization.

Several resources are available for appraising CEO performance in specific types of organizations. For example, John W. Nason's book, *Presidential Assessment,* is a guide to the periodic review of college and university presidents. Although its intent is for use in higher education, it has a great deal of information that is directly transferable to other settings.[9] Similarly, the Girl Scouts of the U.S.A. have done some excellent work on the appraisal of executive directors that can also be useful to other organizations.[10]

In some cases organizations may not have a comprehensive corporate planning process in place or even a written job description for the CEO. It is still possible to appraise the executive's performance. In these cases the board chair and the executive should review the past year's board agenda and minutes and write down any specific goals or expected accomplishments that have been agreed upon (e.g., fund raising goal, budget figures, program and service projections, new programs and activities, etc.). The question then becomes what happened? (Were goals reached? Exceeded? Where was performance short, if at all? Why?) These data combined with feedback from other board members and the board chair's own observations can provide a reasonably accurate and helpful picture of the chief executive's performance during the year.

Regardless of the kind of appraisal used, it is suggested that the results become the major element in recommending a salary adjustment for the chief executive based on merit. The board chair must give leadership to appraisal of the CEO's performance and to any salary adjustment. If the board chair neglects or simply forgets about the CEO's salary adjustment, it can result in an unnecessarily awkward situation.

● **Develop financial resources for achieving goals**

One of the major gaps in planning and management for most nonprofit organizations is the almost complete lack of any long-term financial development strategy. Essentially, such a strategy specifies the organization's overall approach for acquiring and allocating the financial resources necessary to achieve its long range goals. Usually this strategy is developed by a small strategy committee of the board, working jointly with the chief executive officer. Assistance in choosing committee members and in formulating financial development strategies can be obtained in the chapter on "Strategy Development" of the book, *Managing for Impact in Nonprofit Organizations.*"[11]

Although the entire board reviews and finally approves the organization's financial development strategy, the formulation of the strategy is accomplished by a small committee, as previously noted. The entire board is ultimately responsible, however, for obtaining funding to ensure the financial viability of the organization and its programs. Does this mean that board members must fund the organization from their own means? Not at all. It does mean, however, that board members hold the ultimate responsibility for attracting the necessary funding.

I feel strongly that one of the first things that board members need to do is to give themselves. Making an annual contribution—within one's means—is not buying a seat on the board, but it is an important act of commitment. Not to give is simply to declare indifference. Every organization should expect and receive 100 percent participation from its board.[12] In addition, board members should, if possible, participate in annual support efforts by soliciting contributions from others and/or by "opening doors" for potential donors and/or by making presentations for funding to United Ways, corporations and foundations. Some board members find that asking for money is very distasteful, particularly going to a friend or acquaintance to solicit a contribution. As Howe points out, however, board members can assist significantly in fund raising without ever personally soliciting a donation: giving themselves; helping staff in preparation (offering additions to prospect lists, identifying and evaluating prospects, etc.); cultivating prospects; introducing others to make a solicitation visit; accompanying others; writing personal notes, etc. Ensuring that money is available to achieve the organization's goals is a critical task—one that need not be unpleasant—but one that requires the support and help of all board members.

●**Adopt and monitor the agency's operating budget, financial development plan and insurance program**

This particular function must seem very obvious, but I am amazed at the number of nonprofit boards that perfunctorily approve the budget and other financial plans without really knowing the content. Certainly the entire board does not have to be intimately familiar with all details—most boards have budget and finance committees that give continuous oversight to financial matters. However, the board must satisfy itself that the budget is a specification of the resources needed to achieve the organization's goals and objectives. To assist the board, Brian O'Connell suggests that the format for the budget should include at least the following:[13]

> —A narrative summary of the year ending and the year ahead

> —A five-year review of revenues and expenses

> —A comparison of working fund activities and balances for the closing and prior years

> —A proposed budget including, for each line item, the prior year's budget, the prior year's actual and the recommendation for the coming year

Financial evaluation and monitoring is an important part of the board's fiduciary responsibility. As a basis for this kind of monitoring, the staff should prepare a monthly or quarterly budget variance analysis report for the board. A variance analysis compares actual to budgeted revenues and expenses for the current year-to-date period. Management should be required to provide documentation or explanations of significant variances. Although organizations will differ in terms of the significance of variances, a good rule of thumb is to prepare explanations for all variances of more than eight or ten percent.[14]

The board should ensure that an annual financial audit is conducted in accord with the appropriate audit guide of the American Institute of Certified Public Accountants (AICPA) if the organization handles more than $5,000. All nonprofits are required to present a Balance Sheet and a Statement of Revenue, Support and Expenses. Organizations covered by the Voluntary Health and Welfare Audit Guide are also required to present a Statement of Functional Expenses with expenses broken out by administrative, fund raising and program categories.

Lastly, the board must be certain that the agency has in place a comprehensive insurance program to properly protect its physical and economic assets and its people. In today's society the well managed nonprofit also has an effective risk management program—a preventive process that identifies, evaluates and controls sources of possible loss. The First Nonprofit Risk Pooling Trust in Chicago has recently published an excellent resource on risk management and insurance for nonprofit managers.[15]

● **Monitor the achievement of goals and objectives**
The board must keep itself informed and constantly ensure the kind of performance reporting necessary to assess the achievement of goals and objectives. Certainly the financial reporting, noted previously, is an important input for monitoring the fiscal and financial position of the organization. Not all goals and objectives, however, have a fiscal measure, therefore comprehensive *performance* reporting should be required. In all too many cases, nonprofit managers, when requested to report on performance, respond in terms of anecdotal

23

data or broad generalizations. As heartwarming and emotionally compelling as anecdotes may be—neither anecdotes nor generalizations provide an adequate basis for the board to monitor achievement of goals and objectives.

To fulfill its monitoring function the board must require periodic performance reports from the chief executive officer—summaries of performance on all objectives related to long range goals. In addition, the board should conduct an annual update and review session to: 1) review and formulate recommendations for adjusting, as necessary, the organization's long range goals in light of last year's performance and internal and external changes; 2) identify weaknesses in the organization's planning system during the past year and to develop specific corrective actions. Such a session can be completed in about four hours assuming appropriate preparation.[16]

● Perform its legal responsibilities

The board is the legal entity of the organization and therefore it must formally approve all major organizational decisions such as major contracts, acquisitions or sale of real estate, major short-term and all long-term goals and all merger activities, changes in the by-laws and the corporate charter, etc. It is assumed, of course, that approval of these major items is based on appropriate research, consideration and discussion. The board may delegate special power to others, usually the board officers, to sign contracts, open bank accounts, sign checks and engage in other activities as may require board approval.[17]

● Protect the assets of the organization

Properly protecting assets does not mean that the board should not rearrange the organization's assets for maximum productivity. Indeed, ensuring that all resources are maximally used in pursuit of the organization's mission is exemplary stewardship. In doing this, however, the board must be cautious and protect the assets of the organization. I have known some boards that have sold assets (land, buildings and equipment) to balance current operations. To me, depletion of an organization's assets in this way is tantamount to mortgaging the organization's future and is irresponsible board action.

● Form linkages with other community organizations

This involves initiating and supporting collaboration with other community organizations, both public and private, to meet needs that are greater than those that can be met by the organization acting alone.

● Interpret the agency to the community

Many board members want to leave interpretation of the agency to staff with the rationale being that familiar old refrain, "Staff know more about the agency." It's a mistake—board members bring credibility to the interpretation function in a way that is impossible for staff because staff are being paid. It's true that staff are usually better informed about the operating details of the agency, but that is relatively unimportant since interpretation primarily requires a broad understanding and knowledge of the agency. Of even greater importance is the provision of approval and credibility which can best be provided by the board.

● Maintain affiliation and participation in the agency's larger organization and support structure

Many local agencies, but certainly not all, have a larger organization within which they must be or can be affiliated. Although affiliation fees vary, they are usually in the area of one to three percent of the agency's operating revenues which, in the case of larger agencies, can amount to a substantial amount of money. During a money crunch, which unfortunately happens all too frequently with most nonprofits, local boards may resist or even refuse to pay affiliation fees because the money is so desperately needed in the local community. Although I completely understand this dynamic, my experience is that affiliation with a larger entity is invaluable to the local agency, particularly in periods of downsizing or financial crises. In addition to ensuring that

25

all requirements and standards for affiliation are adequately fulfilled, the board should be certain that technical assistance and support is obtained. The board should also actively participate in training and learning opportunities provided by the larger entity and be actively involved in and influence the larger entity in the interest of the agency.

The Individual Board Member

● **Personal Characteristics and Qualifications for Board Members**

All members of the board of directors should be chosen for their personal qualities and should possess either demonstrated qualities of leadership or some potential for leadership. Each person has his or her own list of desirable qualifications for individual board members. Here are the ones that I think are primary:

—Integrity—the ability to know and press for "what is right."[18]

—Enthusiasm about the agency and conviction about its mission. Emerson said it succinctly, "Nothing was ever accomplished without enthusiasm."

—Interest in people—their problems and potentials.

—Demonstrated interest in community service.

—Willingness to commit time, energy and resources to the work of the agency.

—Ability to command community confidence.

—Orientation to the future—always looking ahead.[19]

26

—Special skills, knowledge and expertise that are needed by the agency.

—Ability to represent the community (or major relevant segments) and interpret community needs and views.

—Ability to assess information and make important decisions.

—Courage to state one's views on important issues.

—Willingness to accept and support decisions democratically made.

● **Responsibilities of Individual Board Members**

Individual board members accept a variety of responsibilities and fulfill numerous expectations. To be an effective member of the board, each individual should:

—Be a member or appropriately affiliated with the agency.

—Attend all board meetings and committee meetings, training sessions and special meetings, as appropriate.

—Understand the agency—its mission, goals, objectives, programs and functioning—and believe in it.

—Make decisions on issues, policies, goals and objectives based on careful consideration of facts and all relevant data.

—Participate fully and openly in meetings—sharing insights, ideas and suggestions.

—Keep informed and know what's going on in the agency and never, never hesitate to ask questions or request information.

—Provide counsel, advice and encouragement to staff.

—Give fully and enthusiastically of time, money and expertise, as appropriate.

—Solicit funds, participate in campaigns and open doors for others to raise funds.

—Recruit other volunteers, both policy and program volunteers.

—Serve on committees and accept special assignments as requested and as possible.

—Interpret the agency to the community, be a spokesperson and represent the agency in the community.

Legal Responsibility and Liability of Board Members

Members of boards of directors have a fiduciary relationship to the agency and are accountable for the property entrusted to their care and control. Thus, one should not consider board membership simply an honorary position, but should consent to be a member only if prepared to devote the attention and effort to agency affairs required to fulfill the responsibilities involved. This does not mean that a board member should fear liability for every agency mishap that may occur. To the contrary, a board member is generally protected from liability for errors of judgment as long as actions are responsible and in good faith, with the best interest of the agency as the foremost objective.[20]

Most states have statutes that specify the standard of care required by board members of nonprofit corporations. These statutes usually require that members discharge their duties "in good faith and with that degree of diligence, care and skill which a reasonably prudent person would exercise under similar conditions in like positions." Therefore, to fulfill one's responsibilities as a member of the board and to minimize personal liability, a board member should act in accord with the basic principles of *reasonable prudence and good faith.*[21,22]

The reasonably prudent board member avoids:

... Mismanagement—Taking improper action—misuse of funds in a legal sense (i.e., not complying with federal and state regulations, nonconformance with contracts, etc.).

... Nonmanagement—Not taking action at all; violating the principle of good faith.

... Self-Dealing—Making decisions that promote one's own personal financial interests.

To act in good faith, the reasonably prudent board member should:

... Attend board meetings regularly and make sure that attendance is recorded, including valid reasons for absence.

... Know the agency charter and by-laws and keep informed about agency operations.

... Make sure that a permanent record is maintained of all board minutes and policy decisions.

... Insist on meaningful board meetings with full disclosure of operating results.

... Ensure that minimum statutory or technical requirements are met (filing annual reports, withholding employee taxes, filing IRS form 990).[23]

. . . Decline to vote on transactions in which he or she has a personal financial interest. Avoid any semblance of self-dealing or enrichment.

. . . Require reports at board meetings of all committees of the board.

. . . Ensure that an annual financial audit is conducted by a professional auditing service in accord with the appropriate audit guide (American Institute of Certified Public Accountants) and fully reported to the board.

. . . Adopt and follow sound business policies and practices.

    — Approve annual budget and consistently monitor budget variances with actual revenue and expenditures.

    — Protect the agency's assets.

    — Avoid self-serving policies.

    — See that the agency maintains good credit and financial standing.

    — Obtain competitive bids when prudent.

. . . Be sure that the board uses legal counsel as appropriate and is aware of statutes and regulations, both federal and state, which affect the duties of board members and/or the operations of the agency.

Board Member Job Description

Having a job description for board members can be helpful in several ways. It can be helpful in the recruiting interview to clarify what is involved in board membership. It can be helpful in board orientation as a framework for discussion and as a basis for understanding. Lastly, it can be helpful as a continuous reference document to assist in keeping on track and in board member evaluation.

Exhibit III is a generic job description for a board member. It can be adapted and changed for a particular agency or it can be used for assessing the efficacy of an agency's current job description.

Why Boards Fail

With the kind of specification of board roles, functions and responsibilities in this chapter one might wonder why boards ever fail. I could immodestly assume that boards fail because they have not read and put this material into practice. My experience, however, indicates that there are other major reasons for the failure of boards which I'm hopeful that this chapter and the entire book will assist boards in avoiding. But, why do boards fail?

First, *boards fail because the wrong criteria were used in selecting people to serve.* Board members should not be selected simply because they are nice, friendly people. Neither should they be selected purely on the basis of personal friendships. On the contrary, board members should be selected because they have the attributes, abilities and skills that the agency needs to move forward.

Second, *boards fail because of the inability or reluctance of board members to utilize their talents while serving on the board.* The reasons for multiple: members have not been given responsibility or it is ill

Exhibit III

GENERIC JOB DESCRIPTION

BOARD OF DIRECTORS
Anytown, Any Agency

TITLE: Member, board of directors

PURPOSE: To determine policies, procedures and regulations for the conduct of the agency; to raise funds to finance the organization and its programs; and to monitor organizational performance.

TERM: Three years (unless elected to fill an unexpired term)

MEETING ATTENDANCE: Regularly — Monthly board meetings (10 per year)
                Standing committee (1 or 2 and meetings vary)
                Ad hoc committee (as appointed)
                Special events (as announced)

Occasionally — Agency program events (as a board representative)

RESPONSIBLE TO: Chair, board of directors

RESIGNATION: In writing to the chair, board of directors

RESPONSIBILITIES AND POWERS OF THE BOARD OF DIRECTORS:

1. Establish policies for administering the program and services which are in harmony with the purpose of the agency.

2. Employ the chief executive. (If a branch, approve the selection of the branch executive as nominated by the chief executive)

   Elect other members of the staff upon nomination by the chief executive.

3. Secure funds required for current expenses by mobilizing the entire volunteer and staff forces for active participation in funding efforts.

4. Ensure that the financial affairs of the agency are conducted on a responsible basis in accordance with established policies.

5. Ensure that the property of the agency is maintained in a reasonable state of repair.

SPECIFIC DUTIES OF A MEMBER OF THE BOARD OF DIRECTORS:

1. Attendance at board meetings (participation here as a policy maker and planner is the most important part of the job).

   —Attend regularly and on time.

Exhibit III (*Cont'd*)

—Become well informed (in advance) on all agenda items.

—Contribute knowledge and express points of view based on experience.

—Consider other points of view, make constructive suggestions, and help the board make group decisions reflecting the thinking of the total group.

2. Attendance at meetings of standing committees, as well as any special ad hoc committees to which appointed.

3. Become a financial supporter of the agency at an appropriate level.

4. Assume leadership in agency funding efforts.

5. Assume board leadership responsibilities as requested and as possible (such as committee chairperson, elected officer, etc.).

6. Represent the agency at community events, organizations and with private individuals. Speak proudly and positively.

7. Be informed about agency's programs, policies and services.

8. Be informed about the needs of the community, society and constituents.

defined; board meetings are dull and unproductive; the board chair and the chief executive have already decided on major policies and plans; or inadequate orientation. The list of possibilities could go on ad infinitum. Regardless of the reasons, as Dan H. Fenn found in a national study of corporate executives who serve on nonprofit boards— nearly one half feel underutilized.[24]

Third, *boards fail because of large omissions—they leave undone those things which boards should do.* As emphasized in this chapter, the job of the board is to govern—to formulate policies and plans and employ, support and evaluate the CEO; to ensure that adequate resources are available for implementation; and to monitor progress and provide sanction in the community. All too many boards do not focus on their

33

critical jobs, but become dysfunctionally involved in day-to-day operations that are the province of the staff.

Fourth, *boards fail because strong staff dominate all affairs of the agency.* Boards must insist on maintaining the major board functions as delineated in this chapter and provide a competent chief executive officer who gives able leadership to the staff without infringing on the functions of the board.

Fifth, *boards fail because of ineffective team relationships between the board and staff.* Effective agency functioning appears to be highly reliant on strong relationships between the board and staff. The nature and importance of that partnership is the subject of our next chapter.

NOTES: *Chapter 2*

1. Abbott, Charles C. *Governance—A Guide for Trustees and Directors.* The Cheswick Center, 1979, p. 8.

2. Schoderbek, Peter P. *The Board and Its Responsibilities.* United Way of America, 1983, p. 7.

3. Hardy, James M. *Managing for Impact in Nonprofit Organizations: Corporate Planning Techniques and Applications.* Essex Press, 1984.

4. Chait, Richard P. and Barbara E. Taylor. "Charting the Territory of Nonprofit Boards." *Harvard Business Review*, January–February, 1989, pp. 44–48.

5. Hodgetts, R. M. and M. S. Wortman, Jr. "Decisions at Different Policy Levels" in "Charting the Territory of Nonprofit Boards" by Richard P. Chait and Barbara E. Taylor. *Harvard Business Review*, January–February, 1989, p. 50.

6. O'Connell, Brian. *Recruiting, Encouraging and Evaluating the Chief Staff Officer.* Independent Sector, 1988.

7. Kuenzli, Gary. *Successful Board Leadership.* Management Resource Center YMCA's of Southern California, 1984, pp. 216–218.

8. Hardy, op. cit., pp. 188–192.

9. Nason, John W. *Presidential Assessment.* Association of Governing Boards of Universities and Colleges, 1984.

10. Pruett, M. and D. Wells. *Reviewing and Appraising Performance in Girl Scouting.* Girl Scouts of the U.S.A., 1986.

11. Hardy, op. cit., pp. 103–122.

12. Howe, Fisher. *Fund Raising and the Nonprofit Board Member.* National Center for Nonprofit Boards, 1988.

13. O'Connell, Brian. *Budgeting and Financial Accountability.* Independent Sector, 1988, p. 5.

14. *Management Guide for Arkansas Nonprofit Organizations.* Arkansas Department of Human Services, 1987, pp. 44–45.

15. Stone, Byron and Carol North. *Risk Management and Insurance for Nonprofit Managers.* First Nonprofit Risk Pooling Trust, 1988.

16. Hardy, op. cit., pp. 195–204.

17. *The Responsibilities of a Director of a New York, New Jersey or Connecticut Nonprofit Corporation.* The Volunteer Urban Consulting Group, 1978, p. 6.

18. O'Connell, Brian. *The Role of the Board and Board Members.* Independent Sector, 1988, pp. 9–10.

19. Dayton, Kenneth. *Governance is Governance.* Independent Sector, 1987, p. 12.

20. Weber, Joseph. *Managing the Board of Directors.* The Greater New York Fund, 1975, pp. 6–11.

21. *The Responsibilities of a Nonprofit Organization's Volunteer Board.* Council of Better Business Bureaus, Inc., 1988, pp. 10–16.

22. Kurtz, Daniel L. *Board Liability.* Moyer Bell Limited, 1988, pp. 22–30.

23. Reno, Kyle. *Manual for Board Members of Not-For-Profit Organizations.* Technical Assistance Center, Denver, 1986, p. 6.

24. Fenn, Dan H., Jr. "Executives as Community Volunteers." *Harvard Business Review,* March–April, 1971.

chapter 3.

Volunteer-Staff Relationships

A crucial component in effective functioning of boards and other volunteer groups such as committees, commissions and councils is the relationship which is maintained between these groups and the staff of the agency. Admittedly, the lines differentiating the roles, responsibilities and functions between policy groups and staff are not always absolutely clear and distinct. More often than not, issues have both idea and action components that require policy groups and staff to collaborate. There are, however, fundamental principles that can give guidance to the development of a volunteer-staff partnership that is characterized by interdependence, mutual support and excellence in performance.

The Delicate Balance

A nonprofit organization is a very finely balanced mechanism. The balance is maintained when both board and staff understand and accept their separate roles and the importance of interdependent functioning. Simply stated, *both board and staff must be committed to the idea that working together leads to more effective decisions and actions than working in isolation.*

The balance is contingent upon two main supports in the relationship—trust and need.[1] Each party must make a genuine and sincere effort to understand the other. As noted by Conrad and Glenn, understanding breeds confidence and confidence leads to trust. Trust must be based on the understanding that neither party is primarily interested in self-aggrandizement but rather that both will act responsibly and in the interest of the agency.

Regarding need, I'm convinced that the majority of board and committee volunteers do not really believe that the agency would do just as well if they were not present. Need is substantiated if individuals can clearly see what each group brings to the volunteer-staff partnership that is unique.

Unique Contributions of Board and Committee Members
Among the many positives that policy group members bring to the agency are the following:

- Knowledge and understanding of the needs and potentials of the community.

- Special abilities, skills and insights which the agency could never purchase.

- Influence for attracting financial resources, human resources and public resources.

- Ability to commend the agency to the community and to particular segments of the community.

- Objectivity and the capacity for critical review.

37

- Credibility and community confidence in the agency and its work.

Unique Contributions of Staff
Some of the attributes that staff bring to the agency include:

- Knowledge of the traditions and ideals of the agency and skill in transmitting these into reality.

- Technical skill in agency work, based on training and experience in the field.

- Ability to unite people and to bridge between cultures, particularly in a culturally diverse agency.

- Knowledge of resources that can enlarge the possibilities of agency work and skill in making such resources available.

- Alertness to current and future relevant changes in the larger environment and competence in relating others to the task of meeting them.

- Ability to interpret board planning and policy decisions throughout the agency.

Volunteer-Staff Functions and Responsibilities

In 1929 Arthur Swift completed a research project with social agencies in New York City in which he identified three major functions and corresponding volunteer and staff responsibilities. Swift's basic construct is still evident in many nonprofit organizations today, primarily because of its clarity, brevity and usefulness. I have added to and refined Swift's construct in an effort to provide a useful method for consistently sorting out the tasks in an agency. In addition I have subsumed "planning" within Swift's use of "policy." The following broad delineation of volunteer-staff functions can be used effectively in clarifying particular responsibilities and in effecting a strong volunteer-staff partnership.

Policy Formulation... is the task of both volunteer members of boards and committees and staff members. Policy formulation is a cooperative effort in which each group brings their special insights, experience and skill to bear on the task. It involves the identification of policy needs, the formulation of policy options and consideration of policy options.

Policy Determination... is the responsibility of the board of directors alone. This responsibility derives from the legal status of the board. Board actions establish policies and direction for the total agency.

Policy Implementation... is the responsibility of staff working under the direction of the chief executive officer. Once established, policies are carried out by staff. Volunteers may be involved and assist in implementation, but the CEO is ultimately responsible to the board to see that policies are executed. A special situation arises when a board member is also a direct service or "hands on" volunteer, helping to get a job done. In such cases, the board member must remember that as a direct service volunteer one is serving under the direct supervision of a staff person.[2]

Policy Monitoring... is the responsibility of both volunteer boards and committees and staff members. Staff are responsible for periodic performance reporting on implementation and policy groups are responsible for making judgments concerning the efficacy of implementation and determining future actions as appropriate.

39

Who Does What?

It should be reiterated that in any consideration of volunteer-staff relationships it must always be kept in mind that the chief executive officer is solely responsible for the assignment and supervision of all staff. Board members do not direct and supervise the work of staff members. Board members must always go through the CEO in dealing with staff. In the event staff come directly to a board member with a job complaint or organizational suggestion, the board member should politely but directly refer the staff person to the CEO. Unless these lines of authority are strictly adhered to by all board members, the board cannot legitimately hold the CEO accountable for implementation and for staff performance.

Even with this clarification and with the construct of four key functions discussed earlier, the responsibilities for specific activities in nonprofits is not always distinct and clear. Exhibit I is a listing of forty typical activities carried on in most agencies at one time or another. The items, of course, can be changed or adapted for particular organizations if desired. The instrument is designed to be used with boards and related staff to obtain clarity and agreement regarding board and staff responsibilities and relationships. This can be administered and subsequently discussed in a board meeting or as part of the board's orientation program or in a special board training session. Exhibit II contains the recommended answers for "Who Does What?"[3]

Guiding Principles

The following fundamental principles should be taken into consideration in effecting strong and productive volunteer-staff relationships:

Exhibit I

WHO DOES WHAT?

Board-Staff Responsibilities and Relationships

Instructions: Agency leadership is a partnership of board volunteers and staff. Below are listed some typical actions carried on in most agencies at one time or another. Identify those that are primarily the responsibility of staff by placing an "S" in the blank; those that are primarily the responsibility of board volunteers by placing a "B" in the blank; and those that are primarily a joint responsibility of staff and board by placing a "J" in the blank. Complete all items. Discussion will follow.

PLANNING

1. __ Direct the process of planning
2. __ Provide input for long range goals
3. __ Approve long range goals
4. __ Formulate annual objectives
5. __ Approve annual objectives
6. __ Prepare performance reports on achievement of goals & objectives
7. __ Monitor achievement of goals and objectives

PROGRAM

8. __ Conduct survey of community and/or constituent problems
9. __ Determine fees for a class
10. __ Plan program schedule
11. __ Train volunteer leaders
12. __ Evaluate programs
13. __ Maintain program records; prepare program reports

FINANCE

14. __ Prepare preliminary budget
15. __ Finalize and approve budget
16. __ See that expenditures are within budget during year
17. __ Solicit contributions in current support and/or capital campaigns
18. __ Organize campaign for funds
19. __ Approve expenditures outside authorized budget
20. __ Ensure annual audit of agency

PERSONNEL

21. __ Employ chief executive officer
22. __ Employ other staff
23. __ Direct work of staff
24. __ Conduct performance review with agency program director
25. __ Decision to add staff
26. __ Settle discord among staff

COMMUNITY RELATIONS

27. __ Interpret agency to community
28. __ Write news stories
29. __ Provide agency linkage with other community organizations

BOARD/COMMITTEES

30. __ Appoint committee members
31. __ Call committee chairperson to urge him/her into action
32. __ Promote attendance at board/committee meetings
33. __ Recruit new board members
34. __ Plan agenda for board meetings
35. __ Take minutes at board meetings
36. __ Plan and propose committee organization
37. __ Prepare exhibits, factual material and proposals for board and committees
38. __ Sign legal documents
39. __ Follow-up to ensure implementation of board and committee decisions
40. __ Settle clash between committees

Exhibit II
RECOMMENDED ANSWERS: "WHO DOES WHAT?"

The following answers are based on the concept of primary responsibility. In reality, board and staff members are involved in almost all of the activities.

1. _S_ Directing process (or the way we do planning) as differentiated from content. Specifically, a major responsibility of the CEO.

2. _J_ Both are responsible for input on goals.

3. _B_ Solely a board responsibility.

4. _S_ Board and committees can be helpful.

5. _B_ Responsibility may be delegated by board to branch boards or committees.

6. _S_ Strictly staff preparation.

7. _J_ Works better if joint, but individual responsibilities must be identified.

8. _S_ Board or other volunteers may be helpful.

9. _S_ Within fee policy set by board.

10. _S_ Program operation.

11. _S_ While staff, board may be involved in helping.

12. _B_ May be delegated to committees or task forces, with technical assistance of staff. Rationale: separates ultimate evaluation responsibility from program operational responsibility.

13. _S_ Staff preparation.

14. _S_ Preliminary work.

15. _B_ Final approval is a policy decision.

16. _S_ Management responsibility.

17. _B_ While more appropriate, staff must provide backing.

18. _S_ Management technical responsibility.

19. _B_ Strictly board.

20. _B_ Same as above.

21. _B_ Same as above

22. _S_ Board and committee members consulted, but staff does hiring.

23. _S_ Strictly management function.

24. _S_ Supervisory responsibility, therefore staff.

25. _B_ Policy decision. Usually finalized at time of budget approval.

26. _S_ Management responsibility.

27. _B_ With strong support by staff.

28. _S_ May require board or committee member assistance.

29. _J_ Joint responsibility.

30. _B_ Usually board chair (chief volunteer officer).

31. _B_ Board officers can usually be more effective in prodding chairperson into action.

32. _J_ Best when shared.

33. _B_ Board responsibility with strong staff support.

34. _J_ Best when shared. Board chair and CEO.

35. _S_ Usually staff and reviewed by board secretary and CEO; best when done by support staff.

36. _J_ Best when shared. Usually board chair and CEO.

37. _S_ Staff preparation.

38. _B_ Usually requires one or more board officers.

39. _S_ Staff implementation.

40. _B_ Strictly board function.

42

1. Both parties must be committed to the idea that working together—a partnership—leads to more effective functioning than working in isolation.

2. The relationship should be based on mutual recognition of and respect for the unique and necessary contributions which each group brings to the work of the agency.

3. The relationship should be characterized by mutual trust and openness.

> .. Trust that each will act responsibly and in the best interest of the agency.

> .. Complete openness and sharing of relevant information, feelings, concerns, criticisms and points of view.

4. The board of directors is the responsible legal body of the agency. As such, it selects and employs the chief executive officer and is the legal employer of all on the payroll.

5. Policy, funding, monitoring and sanction responsibilities are functions of the board. Administrative, managerial and program responsibilities are functions of the staff.

6. Volunteer-staff interaction can contribute directly to strong relations. This can be accomplished by annual board-staff planning conferences; providing staff (in addition to the CEO and chief fiscal officer) the opportunity on a planned basis to attend board meetings as observers; and inviting board members to observe staff meetings, particularly those where program reports and considerations are the primary agenda.[4]

7. The board chair is the chief of all policy groups (board and committees).

8. The chief executive officer is the chief of staff. As such, the CEO is responsible for the selection, assignment, training, supervision, performance and dismissal, if necessary, of all employed staff.

Exhibit III, "Dimensions of Excellence," is designed to help board members and staff internalize many of the principles in this chapter. It can be used in a regular board meeting or in a special training session on board/CEO functioning. Exhibit IV is the scoring and instruction sheet for "Dimensions" and Exhibit V is a "Profile" for plotting individual scores as a basis for discussion, clarification, understanding and agreement.

Board Chair—Chief Executive Relationships

A very special and important relationship in agency functioning is that of the board chair and the chief executive. Kenneth Dayton states it emphatically: "I submit that the most crucial relationship in the entire enterprise is that between the CEO and the chairman."[5]

This key relationship is built on the base of mutual trust and confidence. More specifically, these key players need to:

● **Meet regularly on a face-to-face basis**—Meetings should be held at least monthly and probably more often at the beginning of the relationship. It takes time and investment to develop a relationship. The CEO and board chair of one of my client organizations meet weekly for breakfast. In these meetings they take the time to really get into some issues, catch each other up on developments and provide mutual counsel, advice and help. When the chair-elect is selected, this person is included in these critical sessions, thus making a smooth leadership transition. I've talked with several persons over the years who have

Exhibit III
DIMENSIONS OF EXCELLENCE

Agency Board-Chief Executive Functioning

NAME: _____ DATE: _____

Instructions: Place a check mark next to the answer following each statement that best expresses your feeling about the statement. "Not Sure" is a valid answer. Do not enter anything in the boxes to the far right of each page.

DIMENSION I

1. Board members are volunteers with little or no <u>professional</u> skill and insight that is appropriate for agencies.

   AGREE _____   NOT SURE _____   DISAGREE _____

2. Mainly because staff are fulltime they are in a better position than the board to discover and evaluate the community's interests and needs.

   AGREE _____   NOT SURE _____   DISAGREE _____

3. If an agency is having financial problems, it probably has a non-involved, uninformed board.

   AGREE _____   NOT SURE _____   DISAGREE _____

4. Most agencies would run just as well if boards were in an advisory status.

   AGREE _____   NOT SURE _____   DISAGREE _____

5. The credibility of an agency in the community depends upon the board.

   AGREE _____   NOT SURE _____   DISAGREE _____

   TOTAL

45

DIMENSION II

6. There is some information about the agency which is not the business of the board.

   AGREE _____   NOT SURE _____   DISAGREE _____

7. A chief executive should rely on a few board members for decisions, especially those who know the executive well and agree with the agency's direction.

   AGREE _____   NOT SURE _____   DISAGREE _____

8. Chief executives should rarely, if at all, discuss controversial issues with board members or put those issues on agendas.

   AGREE _____   NOT SURE _____   DISAGREE _____

9. Chief executives should "level" with their board members on issues; seek and receive helpful advice.

   AGREE _____   NOT SURE _____   DISAGREE _____

10. Board meetings should basically be information and reporting sessions, as differentiated from sessions dealing with long range planning and policies.

    AGREE _____   NOT SURE _____   DISAGREE _____

TOTAL

<u>*DIMENSION III*</u>

11. The board is responsible for monitoring achievement of the agency's goals and objectives and its performance on budget.

    AGREE _____   NOT SURE _____   DISAGREE _____

12. Having employed the chief executive, the board should supervise, direct and require the executive to submit all decisions for its deliberation.

    AGREE _____   NOT SURE _____   DISAGREE _____

13. The board is responsible for determining long range goals based on need, opportunities and what it thinks the agency should be in the community.

    AGREE _____   NOT SURE _____   DISAGREE _____

14. In actual practice, the board should only ratify staff decisions.

    AGREE _____   NOT SURE _____   DISAGREE _____

15. The board has little responsibility in representing the agency to the community and in preserving the agency's unique role.

    AGREE _____   NOT SURE _____   DISAGREE _____

                                                          TOTAL

47

DIMENSION IV

16. The chief executive is responsible for conducting periodic performance reviews in relationship to achievement of the agency's goals and objectives and reporting the results to the board.

    AGREE _____   NOT SURE _____   DISAGREE _____

17. The chief executive is responsible for preparing agendas for all board and committee meetings since volunteers have little need to be concerned with agendas.

    AGREE _____   NOT SURE _____   DISAGREE _____

18. The chief executive is responsible to his/her board members to help them be successful, proud to be a part of the agency.

    AGREE _____   NOT SURE _____   DISAGREE _____

19. The chief executive is responsible for assuring that all necessary data are available to the board for them to make intelligent decisions.

    AGREE _____   NOT SURE _____   DISAGREE _____

20. The chief executive is responsible for directing the process of planning for the agency.

    AGREE _____   NOT SURE _____   DISAGREE _____

                                                          TOTAL

DIMENSION V

21. The board sets the policy direction for the agency and expects the chief executive to implement those policies.

    AGREE _____   NOT SURE _____   DISAGREE _____

22. The chief executive has no role in the policy formulation process.

    AGREE _____   NOT SURE _____   DISAGREE _____

23. Board members have the responsiblity to fund the policy decisions they make.

    AGREE _____   NOT SURE _____   DISAGREE _____

24. Once the board makes a policy decision, the chief executive's bound by it.

    AGREE _____   NOT SURE _____   DISAGREE _____

25. All professional staff members of the agency are responsible directly to the board for effective performance of their duties.

    AGREE _____   NOT SURE _____   DISAGREE _____

                                                    TOTAL

Exhibit IV

SCORING AND INSTRUCTION SHEET FOR "DIMENSIONS OF EXCELLENCE"

ITEM NO.	POINT VALUE OF ANSWERS		
	AGREE	NOT SURE	DISAGREE
1.	1	3	5
2.	1	3	5
3.	5	3	1
4.	1	3	5
5.	5	3	1
6.	1	3	5
7.	1	3	5
8.	1	3	5
9.	5	3	1
10.	1	3	5
11.	5	3	1
12.	1	3	5
13.	5	3	1
14.	1	3	5
15.	1	3	5
16.	5	3	1
17.	1	3	5
18.	5	3	1
19.	5	3	1
20.	5	3	1
21.	5	3	1
22.	1	3	5
23.	5	3	1
24.	5	3	1
25.	1	3	5

1. Check point value of your answer on the "Dimensions of Excellence" from this sheet.

2. Place point value in box opposite item number on the "Dimensions of Excellence;" add all five boxes on each page and enter total for each individual dimension in box at bottom of the page.

3. Enter the Dimension totals from "Dimensions of Excellence" at bottom of the Profile Sheet.

4. On the line in the center of each Dimension column on the Profile Sheet, place a dot opposite the number on the left of the Profile which corresponds to the number at the bottom of the column.

5. Connect the dots. The resulting graph generally indicates where you are with respect to the five important Dimensions of Agency Board/CEO Functioning.

6. *For Discussion:* Share your Profile Sheet with others in your work group. Identify the Dimensions with greatest differences among group members and refer back to individual items on the "Dimensions of Excellence." Discuss the rationale underlying individual responses and work at obtaining clarity and/or consensus.
    REMEMBER: Focus your discussion on differences of opinion among persons in your work group rather than on whether the above answers are "right" or "wrong."

Exhibit V
PROFILE ON "DIMENSIONS OF EXCELLENCE"

	GREAT	NOT BAD	TAKE ANOTHER LOOK

DIMENSIONS

I. NEED FOR THE BOARD	II. TRUST	III. ROLE OF THE BOARD	IV. ROLE OF THE CHIEF EXECUTIVE	V. BOARD/CEO RELATIONSHIPS

25
24
23
22
21
20
19
18
17
16
15
14
13
12
11
10
9
8
7
6
5

NAME: _____
DATE: _____

Scoring format adapted from Survey of Boards, Institute for Voluntary Organizations, Downers Grove, Illinois

been involved in these weekly sessions and all agree that these meetings were vital and exceedingly useful.

● **Be open, candid and straightforward**—There can be no organizational secrets between the board chair and the chief executive. Both must share the same data base for their leadership to be complementary. Some conversations will undoubtedly be "private" (kept from the public) and others may be "personal" (sharing of unique experiences, background, beliefs, etc.) and these must be honored by all parties.

● **Communicate, communicate, communicate**—The need is for continuous and timely communication. Each person should help the other's involvements to be as surprise-free as possible. Each must be sensitive to the need to return calls quickly and to be available to the other when needed.

● **Share and, hopefully, agree on basic beliefs about people**— Research indicates that a primary requisite for success in organizational functioning is that the board chair and the CEO have a basic belief and confidence in people.[6] *Essentially this belief is that people want to do, can do and will do what needs to be done.* When present, this basic belief permeates the entire organization and leads to real and genuine involvement of people and increased productivity. Indeed, both volunteers and staff perform in accord with their leaders' expectations. It all begins with the board chair and the chief executive sharing their basic beliefs and assumptions about people and striving for agreement.

In meeting together the board chair and chief executive will have many things on which to assist each other and work through and discuss. In addition to the on-going issues and concerns, however, there are some joint responsibilities which must command top leadership attention:

1. Agenda Building—Of particular importance is the development of agendas for board and executive committee meetings, along with the contact and preparatory work which must be accomplished.

2. Committee Structure and Appointments—Specifically, at the beginning of each year the committee structure and composition must be examined to ensure that the committees which are appointed are the ones needed to move the agency ahead and to achieve its goals and objectives. At this time and throughout the year consideration should also be given to the ad hoc groups or task forces that are needed to accomplish specific tasks.

3. Strategic Planning—Priority attention must be given to achieving the organization's long-term goals and particular attention is required in developing strategies that are needed on an organization-wide basis to generate the financial resources over the long term to make this possible.

4. Problem Solving—A whole range of problems and obstacles will arise which need to be solved or that require agreement on the process of resolution.

5. Board Development—All of the items which are discussed in this book under the rubric of board development require the direct leadership of the board chair and the chief executive. If top leadership is not given to developing the agency board of directors, it will simply not occur. Board development requires a significant investment of time and unless the board chair and the chief executive constantly encourage and assist each other in this endeavor, their time is apt to be consumed by more immediate matters. On the other hand, if these two key agency leaders put as much time into developing the board as they do to raising funds and winning community support, they will endow their agencies with one of the most precious assets in the non-profit community.[7] The next chapter is the first of Part Two of this book which will provide assistance to the board chair and the chief

executive in operationalizing the key components of board development.

NOTES: *Chapter 3*

1. Conrad, W. R., Jr. and W. E. Glenn. *The Effective Voluntary Board of Directors*. Swallow Press, 1983, pp. 108–109.

2. Swanson, Andrew. *Building A Better Board*. The Taft Group, 1984, p. 10.

3. Hardy, James M. *A YMCA Tool Kit: Complete Orientation Program for YMCA Board Members*. YMCA of USA, 1980.
Corporate Board Orientation: A Ministry of Service. Volunteers of America, 1986.

4. Weber, Joseph. *Managing the Board of Directors*. The Greater New York Fund, Inc., 1975, p. 17.

5. Dayton, Kenneth N. *Governance Is Governance*. Independent Sector, 1987, p. 8.

6. Hardy, James M. *Managing for Impact in Nonprofit Organizations*. Essex Press, 1984, pp. 23–26.

7. Axelrod, Nancy R. *The Chief Executive's Role in Developing the Nonprofit Board*. National Center for Nonprofit Boards, 1988, pp. 1–2.

Part Two

Components of Board Development

chapter 4.

Assessing and Strengthening The Board of Directors

One of the underlying assumptions of this book is that to be most effective, board development should begin with a comprehensive assessment of individual board members. Unless systematic assessment serves as the basis for board development, development activities will not achieve maximum results for agencies. For example, without systematic assessment, board recruitment might be directed toward recruiting "power" persons or personal acquaintances without regard for total composition of the board and the kinds of persons needed on the board at a particular point in time.

The purpose of this chapter is to present a tested model for systematically assessing members of boards in relationship to eight major factors that contribute to board effectiveness and to provide guidance for taking action based on the assessment. The model yields: 1) an index of each board member's value in relationship to eight factors and their importance for a particular agency; 2) a board profile which indicates the desired proportion of each of the eight factors and the

57

degree to which each of the factors is present in the board. These data can be used for reconstituting the board, identifying and recruiting new board members, conducting orientation and training and as a basis for a variety of other board development activities.

Factors for Assessment

There are eight factors which should be present in varying degrees for agency boards to function effectively.[1,2] These factors constitute skills, experience, knowledge, insight and personal involvement levels that represent the basis for assessment. A brief description of each of the eight major factors follows:

1. **Agency Expertise**—the degree to which the board member understands the agency's purpose, goals, objectives and ways of functioning. This factor is necessary for intelligent board member participation and effective policy formulation.

2. **Management Experience**—the degree to which the board member serves in a top level management position in his or her own organization and is able to constantly strengthen the agency's functioning on the basis of management principles to which the agency subscribes. This factor is important for organizational review and to effect changes needed to keep the agency functioning efficiently. Research indicates that about one fourth of nonprofit board members lack direct managerial experience and that many others—clergy, artists, politicians and physicians—are usually not even management oriented.[3]

3. **Community Involvement**—the quality, number and diversity of the board member's other community interests and involvements. This provides linkage to other community organizations and

can assist the board in identifying priorities that relate to social needs of the community. This factor is beneficial in meeting community needs and effecting collaboration with other agencies.

4. **Recognition/Image**—the degree to which the board member is well known and whose participation on the board has a positive impact on the community's awareness of the agency. This factor is helpful in developing a favorable community image for the agency.

5. **Financial Impact**—the amount of influence of the board member in generating financial support for the agency in the community. Personal wealth of the board member makes a sizable personal contribution possible, but even more importantly, it provides a basis for influencing other support. This factor is important for the agency's financial growth and development.

6. **Agency Commitment**—the degree of involvement (leadership, financial support, participation) of the board member and/or family members in the agency's programs, activities or circumstances. Attendance at board meetings is one measure of commitment. This factor involves the board member having a personal stake in the agency and is important for contribution, continuity and decision outcomes.

7. **Community Representation**—the degree to which the board and its members accurately depict the interests and needs of relevant groups or classes of people in the community. This need may be for either formal representation (delegated authority) or informal representation (membership or communications). This factor is beneficial in adequately obtaining input from relevant community groups or components.

8. **Specific Agency Service**—the degree to which the board member provides extra or specialized agency services and contacts that are helpful to the agency's well being. This includes such items as donation of skilled time, special legal or accounting services, pref-

erential purchasing status, and funding contacts with corporations, foundations or public sources. This factor is helpful in increasing agency efficiency and effectiveness.

The relative importance of the factors for each agency will, of course, vary depending on an agency's current status and its goals, objectives and strategies for the future. Determining the importance weight for each of the factors is a critical element of the model which will be dealt with in detail later in this chapter.

Using the Assessment Model

Assessment Team

It is suggested that the assessment be done by a three-person team composed of the chief executive, board chair and the chair of the nominating or board development committee. Should the agency not have either of these committees, then the board chair-elect or the vice chair of the board can be invited to participate. It is important for the team not to exceed three persons. As individuals, team members should be persons who have a good perspective and a detailed knowledge of the agency—its purpose, goals, objectives and operation; are objective and open; and can make critical judgments. In composing the team, care should be taken to ensure that no person dominates, but that all freely express their opinions, ideas and judgments and that each person gives serious consideration to the inputs of other team members.

Work Climate

The team should meet in a quiet place where there will be no interruptions. Arrangements should be made for all telephone calls, except emergencies, to be held for call-back. In doing this work, it is important for the team to keep in mind the following:

1. The work of the team is confidential. Since the team will be addressing personal functioning areas for each board member, the data must remain solely the property of the team itself. The resultant actions and recommendations agreed upon by the team will be reported as appropriate, but not the evaluation data.

2. Each team member must be very open and forthright. Open sharing of insights and objective assessment by each team member is critical to the success of the procedure.

3. The team must work thoughtfully but expeditiously and discipline itself to stay with the task. Completing the assessment is a huge job. For example, if a board has thirty members, then the team will make 240 different ratings. Consequently, considerable discipline is required to minimize unproductive digressions in the discussions. Care must also be exercised by team members to not become immobilized on particular ratings. If consensus cannot be reached within a reasonable time, it is suggested that the team move on and return to the problematical rating later in its deliberations.

Preparation

In preparing for the first meeting of the assessment team, the chief executive needs to:

1. Reproduce copies for each team member of Exhibits I and II.

2. Prepare a *Matrix for Rating Board Members* (Exhibit III) and reproduce a matrix for each team member. The matrix should list all board members in alphabetical order. Use as many pages as necessary and collate the pages into a complete set for each team member.

3. Compute the average attendance at board meetings during the past year in the following categories: 75% or more; 50–74%; less than 50%.

Exhibit I

A DESCRIPTION OF MAJOR FACTORS

I. AGENCY EXPERTISE (A.E.)

Degree to which the board member understands the agency's purpose, goals, objectives and ways of functioning. Necessary for intelligent board member participation and effective policy formulation.

II. MANAGEMENT EXPERIENCE (M.E.)

Degree to which the board member serves in top level management position in his/her own organization and is able to constantly strengthen the agency's functioning on the basis of management principles to which the agency subscribes. Important for organizational review and to effect changes needed to keep the agency functioning efficiently.

III. COMMUNITY INVOLVEMENT (C.I.)

Quality, number and diversity of the board member's other community interests and involvements. Provides linkage to other community organizations and thereby assists board in identifying priorities that relate to the social needs of the community. Beneficial in meeting community needs and effecting collaboration with other agencies.

IV. RECOGNITION/IMAGE (R.I.)

Degree to which the board member is well known and whose participation on the board has a positive impact on the community's awareness of the agency. Helpful in developing favorable community image for the agency.

V. FINANCIAL IMPACT (F.I.)

Amount of influence of the board member in generating financial support for the agency in the community. Personal wealth of the board member makes a sizable personal contribution possible, but even more importantly, it provides a basis for influencing other support. Important for the agency's financial growth and development.

VI. AGENCY COMMITMENT (A.C.)

Degree of involvement (leadership, financial support, participation) of the board member and/or family members in the agency's programs, activities or circumstances. Attendance at board meetings is one measure of commitment. This factor involves the board member having a personal stake in the agency. Important for contribution, continuity and decision outcomes.

VII. COMMUNITY REPRESENTATION (C.R.)

Degree to which the board and its members accurately depict the interests and needs of relevant groups or classes of people in the community. Need may be for either formal representation (delegated authority) or informal representation (membership or communications). Beneficial in adequately obtaining input from relevant community groups or components.

VIII. SPECIFIC AGENCY SERVICE (S.A.S.)

Degree to which the board member provides extra or specialized agency services and contacts that are helpful to the agency's well being. "SAS" includes such items as donation of skilled time, special legal or accounting services, preferential purchasing status, and funding contacts with corporations, foundations or public sources. Helpful in increasing agency efficiency and effectiveness.

Exhibit II

GUIDE FOR RATING AGENCY BOARD MEMBERS

FACTORS	HIGH 7 – 10 POINTS	MEDIUM 3 – 6 POINTS	LOW 0 – 2 POINTS
I. (A.E.) *Agency Expertise*	Person who clearly understands Agency's purpose, goals, objectives and ways of functioning.	Person who has limited understanding of the Agency, but has served on boards and committees in other agencies.	Person who has had no previous experience with a community agency and little or no understanding of the Agency.
II. (M.E.) *Management Experience*	Person who is in a top management position within his/her company or organization.	Person who carries some responsibility for supervision or management in his/her company or organization.	Person who is a specialist or who is not engaged in management in an organization (doctors, plumbers, teachers, etc.)
III. (C.I.) *Community Involvement*	Person who is an elected official or who participates on several other community boards, councils or commissions.	Person who attends occasional community meetings and probably will work on community events when asked.	Person who prior to joining Agency board left the work of community affairs up to others.
IV. (R.I.) *Recognition/ Image*	Person who is well known in entire community and whose name, picture and/or opinions are frequently in local news media.	Person who is known by a segment of the community and who occasionally has his/her name or opinions published in local papers.	Person who has received little if any public recognition for community involvement or professional contributions.
V. (F.I.) *Financial Impact*	Person whose estimated personal annual income is more than $100,000.	Person whose estimated personal annual income is more than $30,000 and less than $100,000.	Person whose estimated personal annual income is less than $30,000.
VI. (A.C.) *Agency Commitment*	Person who is now or has been involved in Agency activities or circumstances (or whose family members are involved), who contributes regularly, who provides leadership, & who attends 75% or more of board meetings.	Person who is involved in one or more Agency activities or circumstances (or whose family members are involved) and makes regular contributions, but who has not provided direct leadership and who attends between 50 & 74% of board meetings.	Person who has not been involved in Agency activities or circumstances (nor have family members), who does not contribute regularly or at all, and whose average annual attendance at board meetings is less than 50%.
VII. (C.R.) *Community Representation*	Person who has been elected to serve on the Agency's board to represent another community group or component.	Person who belongs to a segment of the community & because of his/her occupation or social activities is concerned with needs that are relevant to the Agency.	Person who neither formally nor informally represents a group in the community that is relevant to the Agency.
VIII. (S.A.S.) *Specific Agency Service*	Person who has technical skills & personally provides needed services to the Agency.	Person who assists in locating materials & manpower and secures donations of services for the Agency.	Person who contributes little time or resources beyond the regularly scheduled board meetings.

Exhibit III

MATRIX FOR RATING BOARD MEMBERS

MAJOR FACTORS	IMPORTANCE WEIGHT	BOARD MEMBERS (Listed alphabetically)										TOTAL FACTOR RATINGS	RELATIVE %
		1.	2.	3.	4.	5.	6.	7.	8.	9.	10.		
I. (A.E.) Agency Expertise													
II. (M.E.) Management Experience													
III. (C.I.) Community Involvement													
IV. (R.I.) Recognition/ Image													
V. (F.I.) Financial Impact													
VI. (A.C.) Agency Commitment													
VII. (C.R.) Community Representation													
VIII. (S.A.S.) Specific Agency Service													
TOTAL WEIGHTED SCORE												TOTAL OF FACTOR RATINGS (above):	100%
Low 1/3 (–) High 1/3 (+)													

4. Briefly review the *Description of Major Factors* (Exhibit I) in relationship to current board members. Although most data will be known by either the chief executive or team members, in some cases it may be necessary to gather information prior to the meeting (i.e., other community involvements of board members). The chief executive should, however, exercise care so that he or she does not become the *sole* information source. Other team members will have information. Use this review only to anticipate possible information gaps and, if necessary, gather the requisite information.

Time Involved

It is suggested that the team plan on two meetings. The purpose of the first meeting is to complete the ratings of each board member on each of the major factors. Experience indicates that this meeting will take approximately three hours. Based on this meeting, the chief executive completes all computations and prepares the reports in accord with the instructions contained in the chapter appendix. The purpose of the second team meeting is to review the analysis and to agree on action steps to be taken. The second meeting will take approximately two hours. It is suggested that the two meetings be scheduled within one week.

Some Limitations

Experience has indicated some limitations in the assessment model that can be either avoided or minimized. Among the most important are:

- **Predetermined Factors.** Although the eight factors are predetermined, they do have both a research and experiential base. It is *not* assumed that all factors have the same degree of importance to each agency. Quite the contrary, it is assumed that the importance of factors will vary depending upon a particular agency's desired future (its goals and objectives) and its current operating status. Consequently, the designation of relative importance weights for each agency, if carefully accomplished, minimizes this limitation.

- **Predetermined Rating Criteria.** The criteria delineated in the *Guide for Rating Agency Board Members* (Exhibit II) may not accurately and totally apply to all agencies. For example, the personal income brackets designated for the Financial Impact Factor may be too high or too low for specific communities. Although it is assumed that the criteria have broad-based application, each criterion should be examined and modified, if necessary, to comply with any extremes or special agency needs.

- **Subjective Manner of Assigning Numerical Ratings.** Making judgments on a numerical scale injects an element of subjectivity into the ratings. This can be minimized by consistently using the *Guide for Rating* (Exhibit II) and by using a consensual decision method among team members in determining the ratings. Although the rating scale is intentionally broad (0–10) to provide for differences, and three categories of criteria are offered (high-medium-low), in some cases a person will not precisely fit any category. In such cases, the team must be flexible and make trade-off judgments to determine the correct category (high-medium-low) and to agree on the numerical rating. The testing of the model has indicated that through consistently applying the criteria in the *Guide for Rating* and being flexible in using trade-offs, the assessment team can function with a high degree of reliability (consistency between ratings) and validity (accuracy of ratings), thus minimizing subjectivity.

Conducting the Assessment and Determining Appropriate Actions[4]

It is suggested that the model be implemented in three separate but highly interrelated steps: Assessment, Computation and Analysis, Action Planning. Instructions, ideas and suggestions for conducting each step follows.

Step One: **Assessment**

This step is the first meeting of the assessment team. The meeting consists of the following items:

1. Setting the Climate—Review with team members the "work climate" items discussed earlier in this chapter.

2. Reviewing Major Factors—Distribute to each member a copy of *A Description of Major Factors* (Exhibit I). Discuss the factors and resolve questions of clarification.

3. Establishing Importance Weights—Distribute the *Matrix for Rating Board Members* (Exhibit III) with all board members listed in alphabetical order. Focus the team's attention on the 2nd column of the matrix titled "Importance Weight" and follow the instructions contained in "Step 1" of Exhibit IV. If necessary, the team may assign some factors the same weight. It should be kept in mind, however, that the more the team differentiates between importance of the eight factors, the more helpful the weighting designations will be.

4. Rating of Board Members—Each team member should have a copy of *Guide for Rating Agency Board Members* (Exhibit II). The team should review the criteria for the first factor (Agency Expertise) and make any changes that are necessary in the criteria to account for special circumstances in the agency or community. Using the criteria and numerical values shown on the *Guide for Rating,* the team should

67

Exhibit IV

INSTRUCTIONS FOR COMPLETING MATRIX

Step 1

As a team review the eight Major Factors, decide which one is most important to your agency at the present time in light of its purpose, goals, objectives and present status. Place a "10" opposite that factor in the second column (Importance Weight) of the matrix. Compare the other seven factors to your first choice and assign each an appropriate number from 1 to 9. You may assign some factors the same number. Ask yourself such questions as, "Is this factor about 80% as important as my first choice?" If so, assign the factor an importance weight of 8. Continue until all eight factors have a relative importance weight in the second column.

Step 2

Using the criteria and numerical values shown on the "Guide for Rating Agency Board Members," rate each board member on each factor. Place the numerical ratings in the upper left hand corner of each box.

Step 3

Multiply the "Importance Weight" (second column) of each factor by the rating of each board member against the factor and enter the resulting number in the small box. An example:

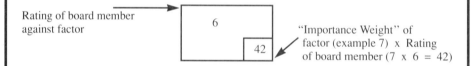

Rating of board member against factor → 6

42

"Importance Weight" of factor (example 7) x Rating of board member (7 x 6 = 42)

Add the numbers vertically in the small boxes for each board member (each column) and enter the total near bottom of page on line titled "Total Weighted Score." Separate the scores into 1/3's (high – medium – low). On the bottom line indicate the low 1/3 by a minus sign (–) and the high 1/3 by a plus sign (+). *This yields an index of each board member's value in relationship to the factors and their importance to your agency.*

Step 4

Add the numerical ratings horizontally that appear in the upper left hand corner of each large box and enter the total in the next to last column to the right of the page titled "Total Factor Ratings." Add the rating scores for all eight factors and enter on the line at lower right hand corner, titled "Total of Factor Ratings (above)." Complete the "Relative %" column for each factor by dividing the "Total Factor Ratings" for each factor by the "Total of Factor Ratings (above)" of all factors. *This yields a comparative index of the degree to which each of the eight factors is present in the board.*

rate each board member on each factor in accord with the instructions contained in "Step 2" of Exhibit IV.

It is very important to start with the first factor by reviewing the criteria (changing, if appropriate) and rating all board members on that factor and then to move to the second factor and continue until all board members have been rated on all eight factors.

     5. Reviewing Importance Weights—Before adjourning, the team should briefly review its "Importance Weights" which appear in the second column of the matrix, and make any changes or revisions which it deems necessary.

Step Two: **Computation and Analysis**
This step takes place between the first and second meetings of the assessment team and consists of making all necessary computations, plotting the board profile (Exhibit V) and preparing copies for use by the team at its second meeting. This preparation should be accomplished by the chief executive.

Instructions for completing the matrix are contained in "Steps 3 and 4" of Exhibit IV. Exhibit VI is an example of a completed matrix on a hypothetical board. When completed, the matrix yields an index of each board member's value in relationship to the factors and their importance to the agency.

Instructions for completing the *Profile of Board of Directors* (Exhibit V) are contained in Exhibit VII. The profile provides a graphic comparison between the degree to which each of the eight factors is present in the board and the degree of importance of the eight factors. The profile can be helpful in identifying the factors that need to receive primary consideration in selecting new board members and in developing an orientation, training and involvement program for strengthening the board.

Exhibit V

PROFILE OF BOARD OF DIRECTORS

FACTORS	RELATIVE PERCENT
I. A.E.	
II. M.E.	
III. C.I.	
IV. R.I.	
V. F.I.	
VI. A.C.	
VII. C.R.	
VIII. S.A.S.	

RELATIVE PERCENT: 0, 2, 4, 6, 8, 10, 12, 14, 16, 18, 20, 22, 24, 26, 28, 30

■ DESIRABLE FACTOR PROPORTION

▨ PRESENT RELATIVE % FOR EACH FACTOR

Exhibit VI
MATRIX FOR RATING BOARD MEMBERS

(Example)

BOARD MEMBERS (Listed alphabetically)

MAJOR FACTORS	IMPORTANCE WEIGHT	1. A.		2. B.		3. C.		4. D.		5. E.		6. F.		7. G.		8. H.		9. I.		10. J.		TOTAL FACTOR RATINGS	RELATIVE %
I. (A.E.) Agency Expertise	8	7	56	6	48	3	24	5	40	8	64	4	32	9	72	9	72	10	80	7	56	68	20%
II. (M.E.) Management Experience	6	2	12	5	30	6	36	8	48	2	12	1	6	10	60	2	12	10	60	9	54	55	16%
III. (C.I.) Community Involvement	7	2	14	2	14	2	14	4	28	7	49	4	28	10	70	7	49	9	63	8	56	55	16%
IV. (R.I.) Recognition/ Image	7	0	0	7	49	0	0	5	35	2	14	0	0	8	56	0	0	8	56	5	35	35	10%
V. (F.I.) Financial Impact	7	0	0	1	7	0	0	4	28	6	42	7	49	7	49	2	14	9	63	5	35	41	12%
VI. (A.C.) Agency Commitment	10	9	90	6	60	5	50	3	30	6	60	4	40	3	30	8	80	8	80	1	10	53	15%
VII. (C.R.) Community Representation	4	0	0	4	16	6	24	0	0	2	8	2	8	0	0	2	8	0	0	0	0	16	4%
VIII. (S.A.S.) Specific Agency Service	3	0	0	9	27	0	0	3	9	0	0	6	18	7	21	0	0	0	0	0	0	25	7%
TOTAL WEIGHTED SCORE		172		251		148		218		249		181		358		235		402		246		TOTAL OF FACTOR RATINGS (above): 348	100%
Low 1/3 (−) High 1/3 (+)		−		+		−						−		+				+					

Exhibit VII

INSTRUCTIONS: "PROFILE OF BOARD OF DIRECTORS"

Compute the "Desirable Factor Proportions" by totaling the "Importance Weight" column (second column of Matrix for Rating Board Members). Divide the "Importance Weight" for each factor by the total of the Importance Weights to get the "Desirable Factor Proportion." Plot this figure on the "Profile of Board of Directors" for each factor by capping the dots at the correct point and connecting the dots downward for each factor. Write the % at the top of the bar and shade the enclosed area.

Next plot the "Relative %" for each factor (last column to extreme right of page on the Matrix for Rating Board Members). Cap and connect the dots downward on the Profile for each factor. Write the % at the top of the bar and crosshatch the enclosed area. The Profile should look something like this:

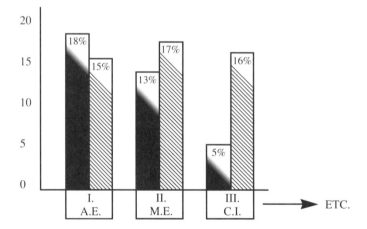

After the chief executive has completed both the profile and the matrix, copies should be made for members of the assessment team as a basis for action planning and for providing a rational approach to board development.

Step Three: **Action Planning**

This step consists of the second meeting of the assessment team. Each member should receive a copy of the completed matrix and profile and a brief explanation of how the computations were made.

After becoming familiar with the two documents, the assessment team should discuss the analysis and obtain consensus on the actions to be taken to strengthen the board. Typically, the assessment team discussion will be in three areas. The following questions are suggested to facilitate the team's identification of appropriate action in each area.

1. Retiring Board Members

   • Based on an examination of the *Matrix for Rating Board Members,* particularly the "Total Weighted Scores: Board Members" and the "low ⅓" (minuses), are there present board members who need to be retired? If so, who are they? Care should be taken at this point by *not* assuming that all board members with a minus need to be replaced. It may very well be that some board members with a minus are low on factor I (Agency Expertise) and/or factor VI (Agency Commitment). If so, the agency itself can take action to strengthen these factors, thereby substantially improving the effectiveness of these particular board members.

   • Can board members that need to be retired be rotated off the board in the near future?

   • If they cannot be rotated off within the next six months, should a direct approach be made pointing out the current

73

need of the agency to have different types of board members? If so, who will make this approach and when?

- Can genuine recognition be provided for board members who will be retired? If so, what form will this recognition take and who will be responsible?

  For further assistance in "retiring" and "recognizing" board members, see chapters 5 and 10, respectively.

2. Selecting and Recruiting New Board Members

- Based on an examination of the *Profile of Board of Directors,* what factors need to be given primary emphasis in considering *new* board, members?

- Who are persons in the community who could bring to the board the combination of desired factors?

- Should other persons or groups be involved in generating names of new board members in light of the most needed factors or in making the decision of who to invite from among several choices? If so, who are these persons or groups? Who will be responsible for obtaining their input? When?

- How will prospective new board members be recruited? Who will be involved in the recruitment of each prospect? When will this be accomplished?

  For further assistance in selecting and recruiting board members, see chapter 5.

3. Orientation, Involvement and Training

- Based on an examination of Factor I (Agency Expertise) and Factor VI (Agency Commitment) in the matrix, should an annual board orientation program be provided? If so, when and who will be responsible?

- Are there individual board members who have a relatively high total weighted score (matrix) but who are relatively low on Factor VI (Agency Commitment)? If so, specifically what can be done with these persons to strengthen their commitment (i.e., individual visits, involvement in committees or projects, increased exposure to programs, etc.)? Who will be responsible for follow-up with these persons and when?

- If Factor VI (Agency Commitment) on the matrix and profile is generally low, could it be that board meetings are boring sessions dominated by dull reports or "treading along in time-honored or ceremonial ruts of minor importance?" If so, what can be done to make board meetings more alive, dynamic, real, important and meaningful? What can be done to increase board member participation, involvement and use of resources in real and important ways? Who will be responsible for implementing these ideas?

- Based on the overall assessment of the board, how is it functioning as a cohesive group? What training should be provided in order to increase the effectiveness of the board's functioning in such areas as: group decision making, listening and communication, group problem solving, conflict resolution, interpersonal relationships, etc.? When should this training be provided and who will be responsible?

For further assistance in board orientation, training, organization and meetings, see chapters 6, 7 and 8.

Concluding Note . . .

As stated at the beginning of this book, board development is continuous, but the starting point is assessment. The use of this model will provide a rational basis for composing a board that's needed by the agency based on its current status and desired future. The model also provides a basis for developing orientation, involvement and training activities designed to overcome recognized deficiencies. It is assumed that the composition of the board should be somewhat fluid; that is, it should be changed periodically based on the kinds of board members that are needed to move the agency ahead in achieving its goals and objectives. Consequently, it is suggested that this model be used by an agency on an annual or at least on a biennial basis.

As noted above, the following chapters are designed to assist an agency in implementing board development interventions based on the results of the agency's own assessment. Utilizing the assessment process and targeted interventions in this way will result in strengthening an agency's board. It will also result in continuous board development.

NOTES: *Chapter 4*

1. Newby, Jack M., Jr. "How to Measure Your Board the Quantitative Way." *Perspective,* September, 1978, pp. 7–11.

2. Vance, Stanley. *The Corporate Director.* Quoted in *Perspective,* 1978.

3. Unterman, Israel and Richard H. Davis. "The Strategy Gap in Not-For-Profits." *Harvard Business Review,* May-June, 1982, p. 31.

4. Hardy, James M. *Assessing and Strengthening the YMCA's Board of Directors.* YMCA of USA South Field Office, 1981, pp. 8–19.

chapter 5.

Retiring and Recruiting Board Members

The assessment process described in detail in chapter 4 is designed to assist agency leadership in recomposing the board. That is, getting clear on: 1) what current members need to be retired and 2) identifying the characteristics of new board members needed by the agency. The purpose of this chapter is to provide further assistance to agency leadership in taking action in these two critical areas.

Retiring Board Members

Board development cannot be done effectively without squarely facing the fact that some board members are nonproductive—they don't contribute or have lost touch—and they must be retired. "Retiring" is a euphemism for weeding, pruning or separating nonproductive members from the governance structure of an agency. It's just

77

as important as recruiting the right people.[1] It's also a lot harder and a job that most nonprofits never deal with because they believe that you can't fire volunteers. That simply is not so. There are many ways to accomplish separation, but basically people who aren't performing must be given the chance to step aside and even asked to make way for others that are needed.[2] Allowing such an unproductive situation to continue does not create the kind of positive and enthusiastic environment that is desirable. It is also a discouraging example for younger volunteers.

There are many ways to subtly prod nonproductive board members or to hint that they might consider resigning. I'm certainly not opposed to trying these indirect methods. My own experience, however, is that a direct, face-to-face, caring conversation between the member and the agency's leadership is the best approach. In such a conversation the leadership can express appreciation for contributions that have been made while pointing out changing conditions and the agency's need for different kinds of board members. My experience is that when a direct, caring and human explanation is given, the nonproductive member is more relieved than hurt. Certainly people know when they have not performed in a responsible manner and they may even be feeling guilty about the situation. In all probability, it will be helpful to remove the burden.

In many instances persons who are unproductive have at some point in their board careers been productive and helpful members. If this is the case, then past contributions should be recognized and honored in an appropriate manner. The point is that the agency's leadership should act in such a way as to make the separation as amicable as possible. But the leadership must act—ignoring nonproductive board members should not be tolerated.

Identifying Prospective Board Members

There are two basic methods for identifying potential board members. They are the *subjective* method which is based primarily on value judgments, and the *objective* method which is based more on an analysis of facts. When used continuously by a nominating committee, or what I prefer to call a board development committee, both methods can be useful. But both also have limitations. For example, when possibilities for board membership are based on subjective measures, there is a tendency to suggest the same people over and over and many capable potential leaders are not found. On the other hand, the more objective method also has limitations. It is frequently difficult to implement and sustain—the limitations being primarily time and resource.

Regardless of the method used, primary consideration must be given to the most needed factors in board composition which were identified in the agency's assessment (chapter 4) and information must be known about these factors and the potential members. Exhibit I is a *Board of Directors Prospect Sheet* that combines information on the eight factors along with personal information that is desired.

One of my client organizations requests all board members to annually complete Exhibit I on as many board prospects as possible. To stimulate individual thinking, the board development committee shares with the board the most needed factors based on their assessment and the desired characteristics of prospective board members. Board members submit their recommendations individually, but are cautioned to not make an inquiry regarding the prospect's willingness to serve. Interest and availability come later in the process. Although this procedure can be quite subjective, it can also be very helpful in identifying prospective board members.

The above procedure can also be used with other groups and individuals who can be excellent nominators: chambers of commerce, United Ways, Junior Leagues, etc.

Exhibit I

BOARD OF DIRECTORS PROSPECT SHEET

PROSPECT'S NAME: _____ ADDRESS: _____

PHONE: _____

BUSINESS/PROFESSION: _____ ADDRESS: _____

PHONE: _____

1. Prospect's familiarity with agency: (agency purpose, goals, functioning, etc.)
   _____
   _____

2. Prospect's management experience: (current position, tenure, past management
   experience, etc.) _____
   _____

3. Prospect's community involvement: (other community groups involved in, leadership
   positions, etc.) _____
   _____

4. Degree to which prospect is well known and recognized: (media attention, public's
   recognition, etc.) _____
   _____

5. Prospect's financial impact: (personal wealth, ability to influence financial support, etc.)
   _____
   _____

6. Prospect's personal stake and interest in agency: (involvement in work of agency, family
   members' involvement in agency programs, background relationship to agency purpose,
   etc. _____
   _____

7. Degree to which prospect represents interests and needs of relevant groups or classes of
   people: (race, gender, age, geography, etc.) _____
   _____

8. Prospect's special talent or expertise needed by agency: (law, public relations,
   accounting, personnel, etc.) _____
   _____

SUGGESTED BY: _____ DATE: _____

Another identification method, called ICL (Identifying Community Leadership), is used by some organizations. It consists of perusing a variety of printed library resources (Dunn and Bradstreet's Million Dollar Directory, Chamber of Commerce listings, newspaper clippings, Foundation Directory, etc.) to develop a gross listing of possible board candidates. A panel of from five to twenty members is then chosen based upon long residency in the community and knowledge of local affairs. The panel, armed with the most desired characteristics of board members derived from the assessment, reduces the gross list to a small listing of the most desirable candidates.[3]

More objective sociological methods of inquiry are available from studies of stratification of power and influence in communities. Several of these approaches can be helpful in identifying prospective board members.[4]

● **The Positional Leadership Approach**—This is perhaps the most logical approach to identification in view of the fact that power, to a large extent, is vested in position. The approach involves two steps: determining the positions that carry substantial authority in a community, and identifying the personalities that hold these positions. This approach has the advantage of being straightforward and relatively simple. However, despite its apparent rationality, it has one severe disadvantage—those persons who work behind the scenes and who may influence those in power positions are not identified.

● **The Reputational Leadership Approach**—In this approach, one person (usually the chief executive officer) interviews knowledgeable persons and asks them to name the most influential persons in the community or other systems. The questions may vary in exact wording, but in essence the question boils down to "Who runs this town?" (community, corporation, church, etc.). This approach, like the positional approach, has the advantage of being simple and easy to administer, but its validity is contingent on the knowledge of the informants.

81

● **The Social Participation Approach**—The focus of this approach is on who belongs to what organizations and who holds what position in an organization. The social participation approach is very effective in determining who participates, but fails to provide information on persons who wield great power in deciding what will be done. Consequently, this approach is seldom used alone.

● **The Personal Influence Approach**—This approach attempts to determine who influences people the most. The approach recognizes that leaders are not necessarily the elite nor are they always designated by formal positions. Because of the difficulty in determining real opinion leaders, this approach is not recommended unless it is used in conjunction with other approaches for validation.

● **The Event Analysis and Decision Making Approach**—This final method involves the careful analysis of the process of decision making which has been used in relation to given issues. Current issues may be selected and followed to a final decision or past issues can be studied on an ex post facto basis to determine who played important roles in bringing about a particular course of action. This is a valuable but very time and resource consuming approach.

My experience indicates that a combination of both objective and subjective methods can be effectively used in identifying potential board members. Regardless of the methods or approaches used, it is important to be aware of two pitfalls in identifying board members. First, the pitfall of tokenism, which is usually based on age, race, gender or ethnic group and results in one person being selected as "representative" of a larger group. To me, it is very insensitive to place a person in this kind of position and can result in a detrimental backlash for the organization. Second, the pitfall of "letterhead" members—obtaining members who cannot or will not be active as board members, but who agree to have their names used by the agency. In my opinion, all members of the board should be fully participating and contributing members. I have known organizations with some "letterhead" board members with resulting resentment and alienation of those board members who attend, work and contribute to the organization. This practice is not only unfair, but also works to the detriment of the agency. Some experts recommend a different strategy. Robert Gale, president of The Association of Governing Boards of Universities and Colleges, says:

> "Generally speaking, it is not advisable to try to recruit someone who has already reached the top of the career ladder. Even if such a person accepts the invitation, he or she is likely to be too busy to contribute. It is better to look for persons who are on their way up and who are willing to work. A valuable talent of nominating committee members is the knack of identifying "comers," those who are moving up rapidly. Such persons, committed to the institution before they reach the top, become investments in the future." [5]

Following the identification of potential board members, the board development committee must reduce the list to those that best bring the desired characteristics to the agency. It may be necessary to place the final listing of candidates in priority order in preparation for contact and recruitment.

Recruiting Board Members

Generally, the way that most nonprofits recruit board members is nothing short of being deplorable. The offhanded manner and the way that contacts are made—using the telephone or mail—send a message to the prospect that neither the agency nor the job is very important. In addition, the comments that are made in an effort to get a quick yes are even more deplorable. I think I've heard them all: "This really won't take much time;" "Don't worry about being out of town so much—just come to meetings when it's convenient;" "Serve on this board and you'll never have to raise money." All of these are degrading to the agency and to the job and responsibilities of being a board member.

Some Tips for Recruiting Board Members

Recruiting board members should be carefully planned and executed. Here are some proven tips that will be helpful:

1. **Carefully chose recruitment team for each prospect.** Generally, a team of two busy people, preferably board members, will make a more favorable impression and be much more successful than a single recruiter. The team of two or perhaps three should be persons who:

. . . Have respect of the subject person. Peer-to-peer or above is the key—but "peers" are not all able. For example, a CEO of a major corporation and a respected author can be peers—equal only in relative esteem.

. . . Have knowledge of the agency—its purpose, goals, objectives, programs and ways of functioning.

. . . Completely understand *why* subject person is being invited to serve—factors desired; person's resources, talents and interests, etc.

2. **Develop a strategy for each prospect.** A separate strategy for each prospect needs to be developed in advance. Essentially, this strategy is based on a melding of the subject person's interests, talents, background and desired factors with the agency's mission, goals, objectives and desired future. Developing an individualized strategy requires homework or research on the subject person and practice. I strongly recommend a training session for all recruiter teams with a major component being a rehearsal or "dry run" for each recruitment

team. Such a "try out" can be invaluable to each team in refining strategy and sharpening its presentation. I'm aware that board members resist such training and rehearsal sessions. When involved in these sessions, however, board members that I have worked with have been unanimous in their praise of the value of this kind of careful preparation.

It must be obvious at this point that quality recruitment requires a considerable investment without any assurance of a positive response. Even when the answer is no, however, the recruitment interview can have positive results, as stated by Cyril Houle in *The Effective Board:*

> "It will be comforting to realize that at least a constructive piece of community relations has been accomplished. The prospective board member will have been given information about the program, will know that he was wanted and will have sensed that the selecting authority (and probably the board itself) knows its business. He is probably an influential person (or else he would not have been invited) and it is important to have influential people aware of the work of the agency or the association."[6]

3. **In making the approach, keep in mind . . .**

. . . Never, never make an approach by telephone or letter—the job is too important. The appointment should be pre-arranged and face-to-face.

. . . Guard against overdependence on flip charts, slides and even handout materials—indepth material and explanations should be given later at the orientation program. Such items as the following, however, will be useful: job description of board member, past board meeting agenda and exhibits, annual report of the agency or other descriptive materials showing agency goals and programs, calendar of board meeting dates and other key events.

. . . Informality is best (if peer or above), with enough time and in a setting condusive to thoughtful and relaxed discussion.

. . . Place emphasis on the agency's future aspirations—its goals and what the agency needs (particularly the subject person's special resources) to move forward in contributing significantly to the lives of people and to the community. This is much more potent than a reiteration of the agency's past accomplishments.

. . . Be honest and straightforward in the presentation— don't make statements for the sake of recruitment that will be regretted at a later date. It is also important for the recruiters to share their own commitment and sense of importance of the agency and its work.

. . . Be sure the presentation is clear, concise and free of agency jargon.

. . . Emphasize the agency's orientation program for new board members and the on-going training program. It is necessary to be specific at this point—dates, times and other attendees. Lack of information about the agency is one of the most frequent reasons given for declining an invitation to serve. Having a comprehensive orientation program, as outlined in the next chapter, that is already scheduled is an effective counter to this major point of resistance.

The Recruiting Interview

The recruiting team should develop its own "agenda" for the interview session, including individual responsibilities. Exhibit II, "Suggested Flow of Recruiting Interview," can be helpful as a general outline in accomplishing this task.[7]

Exhibit II

SUGGESTED FLOW OF RECRUITING INTERVIEW

1. INTRODUCTIONS — to whatever extent is necessary. If chief executive is member of team, this is an excellent opportunity for board members to acquaint the prospect with CEO's background and ability, and reflect on the professional competence of staff.

2. WHY YOU ARE HERE — present the invitation to serve.

3. ABOUT THE AGENCY — its goals, objectives, programs and aspirations. Share your own convictions about the agency and its importance in the community. *Handout:* Annual Report or descriptive brochure.

4. WHAT THE BOARD DOES — the board's authority, organization and operating methods. Share your own experiences as a board member. *Handout:* Board Member Job Description.

5. CURRENT CHALLENGES FACING THE BOARD — what the board is currently involved in that is exciting and interesting. *Handout:* past board agenda and exhibits.

6. WHY, IN PARTICULAR, THIS PERSON IS WANTED ON THE BOARD — individual's special talents, interests, resources and desired factors – the contributions that he or she can make. This kind of personalization is key to a successful approach.

7. TIME AND ENERGY REQUIRED — be sure to answer the question, "How much time will it take?" Point out the orientation program for new board members and its importance. *Handout:* board calendar (meeting dates and events).

8. ASKING/ANSWERING QUESTIONS — this is an opportunity for any questions to be raised. At this point also and/or during the interview, it may be necessary to stimulate interaction and involvement by raising some questions with the subject person: Tell me about your family. What have you enjoyed most in previous volunteer or board assignments? What have you enjoyed least? In your opinion, what are some of the most critical social issues facing our community? What role, if any, do you see for our agency in relationship to these issues? etc.

9. ASK WHEN YOU MAY CALL AGAIN FOR THE DECISION — guard against accepting a "premature no" that can result from requesting an on-the-spot answer. Because of the importance and commitment of the job, it may be necessary to allow "incubation" or thought time, but be sure to follow-up as agreed.

Exhibit III

BOARD MEMBER INFORMATION SHEET

NAME: _____ DATE ELECTED TO BOARD: _____

HOME ADDRESS: _____ PHONE: _____

BUSINESS OR PROFESSION: _____

TITLE: _____ ADDRESS: _____ PHONE: _____

NAME OF SPOUSE: _____

NAMES AND AGES OF CHILDREN: _____
_____

EDUCATION (colleges attended and degrees received): _____
_____

1. Memberships in Associations, Service Clubs, Social Clubs, etc. (include offices held and committees served on): _____
   _____
   _____
   _____

2. Political Offices/Civic Appointments Held: _____
   _____
   _____
   _____

3. Honors and Recognitions Received (include year): _____
   _____
   _____
   _____

4. Other Information (publications authored, major presentations, professional or business accomplishments, etc.): _____
   _____
   _____
   _____

NOTE: Please attach recent glossy photograph.

Finally

Following the final interview session, a member of the recruiting team should write the subject person and express appreciation for the interview. Following the person's formal election to the board and his or her acceptance, the board chair should write a letter of welcome to the person and extend an invitation to attend the orientation program with the chair. The "Board Member Information Sheet" (Exhibit III) can also be sent with this letter.

Public announcements of all new board members' elections should be made. Specifically, news releases should go to: metropolitan media, new board member's community newspaper, new board member's company newsletter, and any appropriate trade, professional or other associated newspapers and magazines.

Recruiting the right people for an agency's board of directors is an exciting but exceptionally time consuming job, if done correctly. It's an investment in the future that's well worth all of the time and effort.

NOTES: Chapter 5

1. Patton, Arch and John C. Baker. "Why Won't Directors Rock the Boat?" *Harvard Business Review*, November–December, 1987, p. 16.

2. O'Connell, Brian. *Finding, Developing and Rewarding Good Board Members.* Independent Sector, 1988, p. 12.

3. Morgan, Mark. "Does Your Board Include Bankers? Here's How to Find Local Leaders." *Perspective*, May, 1989, pp. 13–14.

4. Dolan, Robert. *The Leadership Development Process.* 4-H Volunteer-Staff Development. Undated, pp. 3–5.

5. Gale, Robert. Quoted in *Finding, Developing and Rewarding Good Board Members* by Brian O'Connell. Independent Sector, 1988, p. 7.

6. Houle, Cyril. *The Effective Board.* Association Press, 1960.

7. Kuenzli, Gary. *Successful Board Leadership.* Management Resource Center YMCA's of Southern California, 1984, p. 127.

chapter 6.

Board Orientation and Training

It is not enough to simply recruit board members. They also must be oriented and trained to function effectively. Too often, however, the critical jobs of board orientation and training are neglected because of other pressing duties on the part of agency leaders. The purpose of this chapter is to provide assistance to agency leadership in orientation and continuous training for board members.

The Board Manual

The board manual can serve as an excellent starting point for orienting new board members. The manual provides a single source of information about the agency and, as such, it is an indispensable tool for new board members. Even for veteran board members, the manual serves as a handy reference for the many aspects of the agency coming under continual review.

Although the particular items included in an agency board manual will vary with the type and size of the agency, Exhibit I is a checklist of major items that should be considered.

The most functional format for a board manual is a loose-leaf, three-ring binder, with index tabs. The binder should be attractively imprinted on the cover and index tabs printed for the major sections shown in Exhibit I. This format lends itself to quick reference and to continuous up-dating.

Board Orientation

In reality, the orientation of new board members begins with the recruiting interview. The initial interview is very important, of course, in terms of providing overview information, but it does not go far enough. I recommend that a more formal orientation program for new board members be conducted on an annual basis. The scheduling of this annual session should closely follow the election of new board members. As noted in the last chapter, the orientation should be scheduled far in advance and used as an attractive inducement in recruiting; more specifically, as an antidote to the frequently encountered comment, "But I don't know anything about the agency."

Most organizations never conduct board orientation sessions. In a nationwide study, Dan Fenn found that 45% of those in business who serve on nonprofit boards said, "It takes too much time and trouble to learn what the organization wants and requires of you." Even more striking was the finding that only 15% of board members reported that they had received any formal or informal training or briefing to prepare

91

Exhibit I

CHECKLIST: BOARD OF DIRECTORS' MANUAL

1. Agency Purpose, History and Affiliation

2. Agency Goals and Program
   Long range goals, current objectives, planning process, constituency groupings and program descriptions

3. Basic Documents
   Constitution and by-laws, last annual report, guidelines, regulations, etc.

4. Finance
   Annual budget, balance sheet and current operating statement, last certified audit

5. Organization
   Volunteer and staff

6. Board and Committees
   Board and committee rosters, description of committees, board members' job description, board calendar for coming year, etc.

7. Staff
   Staff roster, personnel policy

8. Minutes

9. Other Information

them for the tasks they were being asked to perform.[1] Indeed, my observation is that even when an orientation session is offered, it is exceedingly dull, boring and consists mainly of a walk-through of the board manual. Agencies need a definitive and participative orientation program for new board members.

Exhibit II contains the design elements for a three-hour board of directors' orientation.[2] The leadership for the orientation consists of the agency's board chair and chief executive as a minimum. Other board or staff members can be added with one person, who is highly skilled in the process of working with groups and knowledgeable about the agency, designated as the facilitator.

When conducted for the first time, the orientation should include all members of the board. In addition, members of board committees who are not members of the board can be invited, if desired. An important part of the orientation is for new board members to feel welcome and have the opportunity to become acquainted with board members who have been serving. Consequently, even on a continuing basis, as many veteran board members as possible should attend the orientation. One of my client organizations assigns the veteran members as hosts for the orientation. This not only gets involvement, but also greatly facilitates the getting acquainted process.

The orientation can be conducted in a board member's home, an appropriate outside meeting place or in the agency's own facilities. If conducted in the agency, a tour of the facilities can be included as part of the orientation. Regardless of where the orientation is conducted, the room should be quiet and comfortable and steps should be taken to preclude interruptions. It is desirable to have seating for groups of six persons around tables to facilitate small group work.

Several parts of the orientation design (Exhibit II) need additional comment.

Exhibit II

DESIGN ELEMENTS: BOARD OF DIRECTORS' ORIENTATION

Purpose:

To provide information and assist in developing insight and understanding essential to performance as a member of the agency's board of directors.

Objectives:

To assist participants in . . .

1. Understanding the basic purpose and underlying philosophy of the agency.

2. Becoming better informed about the goals, programs, organization, financing and operation of the agency.

3. Clarifying the role, functions, responsibilities and relationships of the board of directors.

4. Clarifying the responsibilities of each individual as a member of the board of directors.

Preparatory Materials:

Each participant should receive in advance for review and study a Board of Directors' Manual, loose-leaf with index dividers so that items can be added.

Equipment:

Newsprint pad and easel (flip chart), felt marking pens (one for each group of six persons), projector and screen.

Materials:

Exercise: Looking at the Agency; Exercise: Who Does What?; Reference handout: Board of Directors' Role, Functions and Responsibilities.

Time:

Three hours with a ten minute break (without options).

Major Elements of Session:

5 min.	1.	OPENING SESSION	Chair

— Welcome

— Objectives and flow

25 min.	2.	INTRODUCTORY EXERCISE	Facilitator

30 min.	3.	PRESENTATION: AGENCY'S PURPOSE, PHILOSOPHY AND FUNCTIONING	Audio/Visual

— Questions and response

20 min.	4.	EXERCISE: LOOKING AT THE AGENCY	Facilitator

— Individual completion

— Sharing of responses and discussion

Exhibit II (*Cont'd*)

20 min. 5. MAJOR FUNCTIONS OF THE BOARD
OF DIRECTORS . . . . Facilitator

— Table group task

— Report-outs

— Additions and summary

20 min. 6. RESPONSIBILITIES OF INDIVIDUAL
BOARD MEMBERS . . . . Facilitator

— Table group task

— Report-outs

— Additions and summary

— Comment on principles of reasonable prudence and good faith

30 min. 7. BOARD/STAFF RELATIONSHIPS . . . . Facilitator

— Exercise: Who Does What? (individual completion)

— Group sharing and discussion

— Input: Board/Staff Responsibilities and Relationships

10 min. 8. SUMMARY INPUT . . . . Facilitator

— Role of board

— Dysfunctions in board and staff relationships

— Board/staff partnership

— Handout: Board of Directors' Role, Functions and Responsibilities

10 min. 9. CLOSING SESSION . . . . Chair

— Board calendar of meetings and activities

— Appreciation

— OPTIONS: Installation service; Tour of facilities

● **Introductory Exercise**—The purpose of this part of the orientation is threefold: 1) to help all participants become acquainted; 2) to lower anxiety levels and to help new board members feel more comfortable; and 3) to establish a norm of participation. Most readers will have their own favorite way of beginning this meeting. If not, there are a number of excellent resources that can be helpful.[3]

● **Presentation: Agency Purpose, Philosophy and Functioning**—This segment consists of a presentation about the agency by the chief executive and/or the board chair. It is helpful to use visuals in this presentation (program slides, charts, flip chart displays, etc.). The presentation should include all or most of the following:

—Brief history of the agency

—Purpose, philosophy and goals of the agency

—Description of who the agency serves (constituency, membership)

—Description of the agency's major programs, services and activities

—Organization of the agency (governance and staff)

—Description of facilities and properties

—How the agency is financed

The presenter(s) should make references to appropriate parts of the *Board of Directors' Manual* (which has been received in advance and encourage further study and review).

● **Exercise: Looking at the Agency**—This exercise needs to be developed for each agency. Exhibit III is an example from an agency

Exhibit III

EXAMPLE OF AN ORIENTATION EXERCISE

Exercise: Looking at HOTLINE

Indicate your answers to the following items before discussion:

1. HOTLINE was first organized in: 1958   1971   1978

2. The first suicide and crisis intervention telephone service in the country was organized in:
     1958   1966   1971

3. Since its inception, the basic purpose of HOTLINE has:

     changed little   remained the same   changed greatly

4. Every HOTLINE service in every community requires:

     local building   local board   professional staff

5. HOTLINE is supported financially by (write "1" next to largest source of support, "2" next to second, etc.) . . .

     _____ Contributions   _____ Program Fees
     _____ Endowments   _____ Reserves
     _____ United Way   _____ Public Grants
     _____ Greenwich Health Assn.   _____ Other: _____

6. The ultimate and final authority for HOTLINE is:

     Executive director   Greenwich Health Association
     Local board of directors   Town Department of Health

7. Since its beginning, the program of HOTLINE has:

     changed little   remained the same   expanded greatly

8. Listed below are ten characteristics of a voluntary health agency. All are assumed to be important. Circle the *five* that, in your opinion, are the most important.

     Charitable purpose   Locally financed
     Independent, self-governing   National affiliates
     Inclusive in programs   Professional staff
     Governed by volunteers   Voluntary
     Main stream medicine   Disease orientation

What would your answer be: (for discussion)

1. What would you say if a person who has just heard of HOTLINE for the first time were to ask you, "What is HOTLINE?" What would you tell him or her? Let your own experience join the highlights of our orientation to this point in formulating your statement.

2. You are attending a meeting of a civic group (service club, citizen's meeting, etc.). The group is discussing community needs and apparent duplication of services and solicitations. Another member reminds the group that we have United Way and Infoline. All are aware that you are connected with HOTLINE as a volunteer. They turn to you with the question, "Why isn't HOTLINE part of Infoline or a part of the United Way campaign?" What would you say?

called HOTLINE. It is reproduced with permission and hopefully will be helpful to readers in developing a similar kind of exercise for their agencies. In the orientation when each person has completed the exercise, the correct answers should be shared and time spent in participant responses to the two discussion situations.

● **Major Functions of the Board and Responsibilities of Individual Board Members**—These two questions, "What are the major functions of the board of directors as a total group?" and "What are the responsibilities of individual members?", should be worked on separately by each table group for about ten minutes and reported-out on large newsprint sheets. Following report-outs, the facilitator provides additions and a summary from the material in chapter 2. A handout, *Board of Directors' Role, Functions and Responsibilities*, can be easily developed from the material in chapter 2 for distribution following the final session.

● **Board/Staff Relationship**—The exercise, "Who Does What?", contained in chapter 3, along with the recommended answers, is the centerpiece of this particular segment of the orientation.

Finally, if possible in the chosen setting, the orientation program should include an informal meal. This can add substantially to the fellowship and enjoyment of the occasion.

Board Training

All too often once new members are oriented and hopefully integrated into the mainstream of the agency, there is little effort expended on further board training. Emphasis seems to shift to performing various assignments rather than to continuous development and training. While such assignments are an important part of development, attention must also be given to broadening the experiences of board members.[4]

I recall with great warmth and considerable satisfaction the work of a national policy group to which I was related as the executive. One of the members, an able CEO of a Fortune 500 company, frequently told me and many others that he learned more about management and people as a member of that group than he learned from all of the management training in his business. Undoubtedly, he was overly complimentary, but the point is that the experience of serving was learningful for him because we gave serious and continuous attention to training. I feel strongly that persons who serve on boards and committees should not only give, but they should also be recipients of value. Yes, I know that members receive the satisfaction and the prestige of significantly contributing to the community and to people. But I think board members should also have the opportunity to acquire knowledge, understanding, insight and skills that are valuable not only in their service capacity to the agency, but also of value in their living and service to society. Board training can be a primary mechanism for this kind of continuous learning.

Continuous learning can take place, of course, in a variety of ways. Although board and committee meetings are designed to conduct the work of the board, they can also be a powerful stimulus for learning and a force for informal continuing education. In these meetings consideration should be given to:

- Including a monthly report of the chief executive—a review of recent successes and progress and the stimulating challenges ahead.

- Interpretation of the agency's program and projects, using program staff, volunteer leaders and participants to conduct interviews, demonstrate techniques and/or explain what is happening as a result of board efforts.

99

- Making essential reports and statistics communicate the life and vitality of the agency.

- Visits to observe special projects, programs and activities and increase the fellowship of the board.

- Inviting special speakers, experts or representatives outside of the local agency (i.e., national or regional field staff or volunteers) to broaden the board's perspective of the agency.

Agency leadership should also be constantly searching for methods to develop the potential of board members. This includes appointments to task forces and ad hoc groups, rotating committee assignments and leadership roles, matching special challenges to individual talents and skills, and developing new special assignments.[5]

All of the above activities will assist in continuing board education and should be pursued. In addition, however, the agency should have an on-going board training program that is more structured and perhaps even formalized. Exhibit IV, "Assessment of Board Member Training Needs," is designed for use by an agency's board development committee as the basis for formulating a board training program. It is suggested that Exhibit IV be administered to all board members and completed at a regular meeting near the beginning of a "board year" (i.e., soon after the election of new members and following the annual orientation program). The completed assessment sheets can then be tabulated to produce mean (average) scores for each of the training needs, along with the most convenient and desirable meeting times. These data can then be used by the board development committee in making a decision regarding the training modules to be conducted during the coming year and the dates and times. Most agencies will have two or three training modules presented each year.

As indicated in Exhibit IV, the maximum time for any module is three hours and some can be effectively conducted in even less time.

Exhibit IV

ASSESSMENT OF BOARD MEMBER TRAINING NEEDS

Purpose of the Assessment

The results of this assessment will be used by the board development committee as a basis for selecting training modules for the board of directors that will be conducted during the coming year. The modules that are finally chosen will reflect he training needs of the largest number of board members. The modules will be designed to increase the effectiveness of both individual board members and the board as a whole. It is assumed that most modules will require up to three hours to conduct, although some may require less time.

Instructions:

<u>FIRST</u> – Rate the importance of each training need for yourself by placing a check (✔) in one of the five spaces in column 1 that best expresses your assessment according to the following scale:

> 1 = Not Important at All
> 2 = Minimally Important
> 3 = Moderately Important
> 4 = Considerably Important
> 5 = Very Important

<u>SECOND</u> – Select the *three* most important training needs and rank these three in column 2 according to importance (i.e., place a "1" in column 2 opposite the most important training need for yourself; a "2" opposite the second most important; and a "3" opposite the third most important training need.)

<u>THIRD</u> – Indicate your timing preference for the selected modules and provide other comments by completing the final three items on page 3.

THANKS FOR YOUR HELP

YOUR NAME: _____

TRAINING NEEDS	COLUMN 1 IMPORTANCE RATING					COLUMN 2 RANKING OF 3 TOP NEEDS
	1.	2.	3.	4.	5.	
KNOWLEDGE AND UNDERSTANDING:						
1. Conflict Resolution						
2. Collaborating with Other Organizations						
3. Comprehensive Corporate Planning for Nonprofits						
4. Future Social Issues and Trends						
5. Legal Responsibility and Liability of Board Members						
6. Understanding and Appreciating Cultural Pluralism						
7. Value Clarification						
SKILLS:						
8. Analyzing Nonprofit Financial Statements						
9. Appraising Chief Executive's Performance						
10. Communication Skills						
11. Creative Problem Solving Skills						

TRAINING NEEDS	COLUMN 1 IMPORTANCE RATING					COLUMN 2 RANKING OF 3 TOP NEEDS
	1.	2.	3.	4.	5.	
SKILLS (continued):						
12. Formulating Financial Development Strategies						
13. Group Decision Making Techniques						
14. Interpersonal Effectiveness						
15. Interpreting the Agency						
16. Involvement Skills						
17. Listening Skills						
18. Making Clear and Concise Presentations						
19. Monitoring Achievement of Goals and Objectives						
20. Team Building Skills						
21. Others (specify):						

1. Assuming that most training modules will take approximately three hours, which DAY OF THE WEEK is most desirable and convenient for you?   (CIRCLE)

   Sunday   Monday   Tuesday   Wednesday   Thursday   Friday   Saturday

2. Which TIME OF THE DAY is most desirable and convenient for you? (CIRCLE)

   Morning (9 a.m. – 12 noon)   Afternoon (2 p.m. – 5 p.m.)   Evening (7 p.m. – 10 p.m.)

3. Other comments and suggestions regarding board training modules:

Indeed, some modules might be conducted as part of a regular board meeting. In addition to timing, the board development committee needs to decide on the leadership for each module. Skilled leadership may be recruited from the board or in the community. In some cases, the committee may go outside of the community for special leadership, although these instances will probably be the exception.

It is, of course, very important for the modules to be scheduled, with the best leadership available, for the year and announced to the board when finalized. To ensure desired attendance, ample lead time must be provided for busy board members.

In designing modules to meet particular training needs it is recommended that the training techniques of choice be those with the most active participant involvement. It has been shown that people retain:[6]

    —20% of what they read

    —20% of what they hear

    —30% of what they see

    —50% of what they see and hear

    —70% of what they say

    —90% of what they see, hear and do

Using creative techniques that meaningfully involve board members will result in board training that contributes to the growth and development of individual board members and to the effectiveness of the board of directors on a whole. In short—board training is critical for continuous renewal of people and of the agency.

NOTES: Chapter 6

1. Fenn, Dan H., Jr. "Executives As Community Volunteers." *Harvard Business Review,* March–April, 1971.

2. Hardy, James M. *A YMCA Tool Kit: Complete Orientation Program for YMCA Board Members.* YMCA of the USA, 1980.

3. Forbess-Greene, Sue. *The Encyclopedia of Icebreakers.* Applied Skills Press, 1980.

4. Schoderbek, Peter P. *The Board and Its Responsibilities.* United Way of America, 1983, p. 7.

5. Kuenzli, Gary. *Successful Board Leadership.* Management Resource Center YMCA's of Southern California, 1984, pp. 129–130.

6. Munson, Mary K. *Educational Methods and Techniques.* University of Illinois 4-H Youth, 1987.

chapter 7.

Board Organization and Functioning

The optimal size of agency boards continues to be a subject that stimulates long and vigorous debate among nonprofit theorists and practitioners alike. Similarly, the frequency of meetings, terms of office, committee organization, advisory boards and ancillary groups are subjects that garner diverse opinions. The purpose of this chapter is to provide guidance for agency leadership in these and other organizational matters that, hopefully, will improve the functioning of the agency's board and committees.

Effective Board Functioning

● **Board Size**—Almost all newly elected business persons that I have known who serve on nonprofit boards are convinced that their organization's board and committees are much too large to be efficient and effective. Their judgments are supported by experience from the profit world. A Conference Board study found that the median board size in profit organizations is in the 10–15 member range.[1] Most management specialists are also proponents of narrowing down to the smallest number those who will be involved in decisions. There is no question that a few people making decisions for the whole organization is efficient in a business organization. However, as Brian O'Connell says, ". . . if decisions are going to have to be sold to those who will be affected in the community or in other parts of the organization— and if there is no strong legislative or line authority for requiring compliance—then even businessmen begin to learn that the shortest route to making the right decisions and having them carried out is via a process of maximum feasible involvement."[2] Simply stated, nonprofit organizations need more linkage to other groups and they need a broader base of involvement and "ownership" than do most business organizations.

My experience indicates that few nonprofits can operate effectively with a board that has less than twenty active members. Even fewer can function well with a board larger than fifty. Joseph Weber suggests that 30–36 is an optimum size.[3] Harleigh B. Trecker reports that his studies indicate that the average size is indeed thirty-three members.[4]

Obviously there is no exact number or perfect size for a nonprofit board. In making the judgment, however, there are some matters for consideration:[5]

The board is too LARGE if . . .

> . . . It cannot act as an effective deliberative body—cannot meet and make decisions.

> . . . The quality of deliberations is endangered.

> . . . Personal involvement decreases—members fail to assume their responsibilities.

107

... Meetings become less frequent.

... Quality of members declines.

... Satisfaction of members declines.

... An "inner board" is created to make decisions—oftentimes called an "executive committee."

On the other hand, the board is too SMALL if . . .

... Adequate representation from the community or the constituency cannot be provided.

... It becomes too closely knit or paralyzed by fractionalism.

... Adequate fund raising cannot be accomplished.

... Breadth of necessary resources is not available.

... It cannot divide into sufficient numbers of sub-groups (committees, task forces, etc.) for study of specific issues or areas.

● **Frequency of Meetings**—Board meetings should be scheduled not less than six times a year and may be held as frequently as ten times a year or once a month. Many organizations meet monthly from September through June, or ten times during the year due to erratic schedules and vacations during July and August. I've known some nonprofits that held board meetings on a quarterly basis, with the result being an unhealthy over-reliance on the executive committee and staff.

It is desirable to have board meetings at regular times (e.g., third Monday of each month) and to distribute the schedule of meetings a year in advance. In addition, about two weeks before each meeting members should receive a notice of the meeting, a preliminary agenda, items for preparatory study and a response card on which they may indicate their attendance plans. Members planning to attend should receive a reminder call on the day of the meeting.

● **Terms of Service**—I'm a firm believer that boards need the stimulus of regular and planned change in membership. I also believe that members need the assurance that board service will not go on until burn-out or exhaustion takes over. The by-laws of many organizations provide for a systematic rotation of board members. A fairly common and desirable plan is to set the term of service for three years, with an option to renew for an additional term, based on a mutually satisfactory experience. In cases where two consecutive terms have been served, members usually must go off the board for at least one year prior to being considered for re-election. Such plans ensure membership change, a flow of new resources and contribute to on-going board renewal while also providing for continuity and stability.

● **Minutes**—It is very important that accurate minutes of all meetings of the board and its committees be kept. Minutes are the reference points for future questions and serve as a major mechanism for continuity of effort. In nonprofit corners, there is much debate about who keeps the minutes. It must be recognized that the person who takes minutes does not have an opportunity to fully participate in the deliberations of the board or committee. Consequently, if at all possible, it is recommended that a competent staff secretary be assigned to take minutes. Prior to distribution, a draft of the minutes should be reviewed and approved by the related executive staff person and by the group's secretary. To be helpful, minutes should be concise but complete and should be distributed to all members within a week following the meeting.

● **Officers**—Most boards function effectively with a president (or chair), one or, at the most, two vice presidents, a secretary and a treasurer.[6] More officers than these can rarely be justified, and then

109

in only very large organizations. Although an employed officer of the corporation, the chief executive officer should function as the staff person related to the board and should not be a member of the board. Many funding organizations, including most United Ways, generally discourage or even prohibit paid staff from serving on the board.[7]

Just as board members' terms should be limited, I think volunteer board officers' terms should also be limited. There is increasing acceptance of the fact that one year is rarely long enough for key officers to serve and that more than three years is probably too long. A client organization of mine had a board chair that served for sixteen consecutive years and even though he was an exceptionally able person, he became stale and nonproductive long before his retirement. Andrew Swanson suggests that officers be elected to one-year terms, with re-election to a second and a third one-year term being permissible.

Branch Boards in Metropolitan Agencies

Many metropolitan agencies are organized to serve a total metropolitan area through branches that are responsible for developing program and support in specific geographical areas. In most cases, branches have special volunteer groups (variously designated as branch boards of managers, committees of management, branch operating boards, etc.) that have been delegated the responsibility for the operation of a particular unit of the agency by the metropolitan board of directors. In some cases, confusion and even conflict are evident in terms of the relative authority, responsibility and functions of the metropolitan (corporate) board of directors and the branch board. In these situations, it is important to recognize that:

- The agency in a metropolitan area is one corporation and the metropolitan board of directors is responsible for the total agency.

- The metropolitan board of directors delegates to a branch board the responsibility for the operation of the branch unit.

- The branch board is responsible to the metropolitan board of directors for the operation of the branch.

Exhibit I is an outline of the role of the metropolitan (corporate) board of directors and branch boards in relation to some of the major functional areas that are of concern to most metropolitan nonprofit organizations.[8] Hopefully, Exhibit I will assist those in large metropolitan agencies in understanding the responsibilities and relationships of these two important policy groups—corporate boards and branch boards.

Advisory Boards and Auxiliary Groups

Other boards are sometimes appointed by an agency's board of directors to carry out specific functions or special programs. Although frequently very important in the life of an agency, these so called boards are substantially different from the board of directors. The essential difference is that auxiliary groups do not have the governing powers and responsibilities of the board which appointed them.

To reduce confusion, I recommend that boards of directors be very discriminating in giving the title of "board" to ancillary groups. I think it is desirable to call a branch or operating unit policy group a board,

111

Exhibit I

METROPOLITAN ORGANIZATION: BOARD RESPONSIBILITIES AND RELATIONSHIPS

FUNCTIONAL AREA	METROPOLITAN (CORPORATE) BOARD OF DIRECTORS	BRANCH BOARD
1. *Authority*	Granted by charter, Articles of Incorporation and by-laws. May enter into contractual arrangements.	Assigned by metropolitan board. Cannot enter into contractual obligations.
2. *Policies*	Establishes all general policies for the metropolitan organization.	Determines matters of policy for branch, within the general policies of the metropolitan organization.
3. *Planning*	Establishes the metropolitan organization's long range goals; develops long range strategies; approves or delegates approval of annual objectives.	Provides input for metropolitan goals based on branch needs and potentials; approves annual branch objectives to achieve goals, and recommends these to metropolitan board of directors.
4. *Monitoring*	Monitors goal achievement and annually reviews goals; reports to membership and community.	Monitors achievement of branch objectives; reports to metropolitan board, branch members and community.
5. *Land, Buildings and Equipment*	Holds title to all properties. Determines general standards for maintenance.	Owns no property. Maintains branch property in accord with standards. Alerts metropolitan board to insurance needs.
6. *Financing*	Responsible for financing total metropolitan organization and for administration and allocation of endowment funds.	Responsible for assigned share of organization budget (income and expense). Encourages endowment funds but has no authority over expenditures.
	Determines annual organization budget.	Recommends annual branch budget.
	Arranges for annual audit.	None.
	Negotiates with United Way and other funding sources for organization allocation; allocates share to branches.	Submits branch request and rationale for subsidy.
	Allocates emergency loans to branches for capital repairs.	Requests emergency loans for capital repairs.

Exhibit I (*Cont'd*)

FUNCTIONAL AREA	METROPOLITAN (CORPORATE) BOARD OF DIRECTORS	BRANCH BOARD
Financing (cont.)	Provides service of metropolitan business office (accounting, reporting, banking, purchasing, etc.)	Provides for handling branch funds in accord with general policies.
7. *Program*	Sets general organization program thrusts, as part of goals, and related policies. Coordinates and sets general standards.	Determines branch program and policies based on community needs and organization program thrusts. Promotes program participation. Conducts all branch program in accord with general standards.
	Gives leadership to interbranch activities.	Assists with inter-branch activities.
	Provides standards for program leadership and resources for leadership training.	Recruits program leaders and provides appropriate training.
8. *Staffing*	Employs chief executive officer.	Branch executive employed by CEO, in consultation with branch.
	Provides personnel services for all branches.	Serves as consultant group when branch is concerned.
9. *Relationships*	Represents organization at regional, national and international events.	Sends delegates to represent branch at regional, national and international events.
	Represents organization in general community and organizational affiliations.	Represents branch in neighborhood or local community affiliations.
	Responsible for general city-wide public relations and coordination among branches.	Responsible for branch public relations.
	Provides legal counsel for branches.	Alerts metropolitan board to legal needs.

113

as previously discussed. It may also be desirable, for the purpose of prestige and stature, to call a high level advisory group an "advisory board." However, an organization that uses the term indiscriminately will probably have groups that assume power and authority that they are neither entitled nor intended to have.

There are all kinds of auxiliary groups that can be appointed but there are two that I have found to be extremely valuable to most agencies—advisory boards and program advisory councils. Each merits further comment.

● **Advisory Boards**—These groups are usually composed of highly respected men and women who are considered key opinion makers and influential citizens in the community. For the agency, appointing such persons to an advisory board can be a way of maintaining the interest and resources of desired people after they have retired from service on the board of directors. It can also be a mechanism for relating influential people to the agency who either cannot or do not desire to serve on the board of directors and attend regular meetings of the board and its committees, but who do support the agency and what it is striving to accomplish and want to contribute to its well-being.

Advisory boards provide counsel and guidance to the officers of the board and directors and to the chief executive officer regarding the effective functioning of the agency. It must be made clear, however, that the advisory board has no governing authority and neither the board of directors nor the staff is compelled to follow the advice that is given.

In general, advisory boards are asked to do the following:

- Keep informed about the agency's mission, goals, programs and development.

- Interpret the agency within their circle of influence.

114

- Share their ideas about the growth and improvement of the agency.

- Assist in special problem solving for the agency.

- Participate in fund raising efforts.

Usually advisory boards hold only one meeting annually, although members are invited to attend any meeting of the board of directors and they receive all board meeting announcements, agendas, exhibits and materials. Members are also kept informed by other mailings (newsletters, bulletins, brochures, etc.) and by one-on-one briefings during the year conducted by members of the regular board of directors and staff.

An advisory board can be of immeasurable value—especially one that consists of a select group of people who, by reason of their background and community position, can provide the agency with special counsel and guidance not readily available on the board of directors.

● **Program Advisory Councils**—These groups tend to be as large or even larger than regular boards of directors. They are usually composed of: 1) representatives of different groups that the agency serves or desires to serve (based on gender, race, age, ethnic background, geography, etc.); 2) persons who are current program participants, leaders or families of participants. Program advisory councils provide counsel and guidance to officers of the board of directors, members of the program committee and staff regarding the effectiveness of agency programs and services. As with the advisory boards, program advisory councils have no governing authority.

In general, program advisory councils are asked to:

- Keep informed of the agency's mission, programs and services.

- Identify unmet community needs that are within the purview of the agency's mission and expertise.

115

- Provide ideas, suggestions and inputs for new program development.

- Assist in evaluating specific programs and services by providing data, visiting programs and providing observations, and deriving implications and findings from data.

- Test program ideas—through reaction and/or field testing.

- Interpret the agency within their circle of influence.

Program advisory councils usually meet monthly or even bi-monthly. Program staff always meet with councils and provide staff support and assistance.

Program advisory councils offer a variety of advantages to nonprofit organizations, but most of all they: provide a way of constantly keeping the agency's programs and services relevant to the needs and interests of desired constituencies; and provide an important "voice" for community people to be heard and to influence programs and services that affect their lives.

Committees of the Board

A committee is a group of volunteers duly appointed to perform a specific task within a given area. In recent years committees have taken a beating by everyone from comedians to management experts. You probably have your favorite one-liner about committees. Here are some of mine, authored at some point in time by different wags who must remain anonymous:

> —A committee is an assemblage of the unwilling, deciding the unnecessary, at the request of the uncaring.

116

—A camel is a horse put together by a committee.

—The best committee has three members—with two always out of town.

—A committee is a collection of individuals who separately do nothing and together decide that nothing can be done.

In spite of the humor and wise remarks, committees are important—they represent the major method of organizing the work of boards and a way of getting the board's job done. It should be kept in mind always, however, that the major task of most committees is *policy formulation* while *policy determination* is the responsibility of the board of directors.

● **Number of Committees**—It seems to me that most nonprofits have far too many standing committees and they are "repeaters"—they reappear every year. I don't think it's neccesary and it may not be possible to operate effectively with more than four to six standing committees. Having more runs the risk of spreading the board and staff resources too thin and they may end up stumbling over each other. I think most agencies need the following standing committees:

1. Program Committee

2. Budget and Finance Committee

3. Strategy Development Committee (dealing primarily with long-term financial development strategy)

4. Property Management Committee (if the agency holds property to any large extent)

5. Board Development Committee

There are, of course, numerous other possibilities, most of which can be appointed as ad hoc committees: personnel/employee relations;

117

public relations/marketing; capital development; corporate planning; etc. Ad hoc groups (task forces, temporary teams or project groups) are formed to accomplish specific tasks and are of short and pre-determined duration. I'm a great proponent of ad hoc groups and "temporary systems" that disband when their specific tasks have been accomplished.

Readers may notice in the above listing the absence of an executive committee. It may be necessary and important to a particular agency to have an executive committee that can act between meetings of the board of directors. This should be given serious consideration, however, because there are very real dangers in having an executive committee. In all too many cases, executive committees act in place of boards and risk making the board, in perception if not in fact, a useless appendage that functions only as a rubber stamp.

● **Size of Committees**—Committees must be large enough to carry out the assigned work with a fair sharing of responsibilities, but small enough to allow for ample involvement and deliberation. Many experts suggest a range of from three to nine members. I have found that the "magic number is seven, plus or minus two." In other words, the best range is from five to nine members, with seven being the ideal.

Regardless of the exact number, committees need to be large enough . . .

—so the loss or absence of a member can be tolerated.

—to permit a diversity of opinions and ideas.

On the other hand, committees must be small enough . . .

—so the absence of a member does not go unnoticed.

—so that all members are intimately involved.

—to allow everyone the opportunity to participate fully and to use consensual decision making without unduly extending the meeting time.

● **Advantages of Committees**—Practically everyone has been a member of a committee at one time or another when the effort has been unproductive and a waste of time. Unfortunately, this has been too frequently the case and has caused many busy board members to question the viability of committees. However, experience indicates that some very real advantages accrue to agencies that have an effective committee organization. Among the most important benefits are:

● It relieves board meetings of many routine matters which can be handled by responsible committees.

● It maximizes the opportunities for use of board member resources and involvement through detailed work on worthy tasks.

● It provides the board the opportunity to use special resources of agency members or supporters that may not be resident in the board itself, since committees are not limited to board members.

● It broadens the base of "ownership" of the agency's work and increases support for implementation.

● It improves the quality of policy formulation and problem solving recommendations through small group work that allows careful and detailed consideration of data, issues and alternatives.

● It ensures that all essential factors in carrying out the agency's work are given adequate consideration.

119

● **Conditions for Effective Committees**—Both experience and research indicate that committee work is effective, productive and satisfying to members when:

- There is a clear role definition of the committee—what the committee and its members are supposed to do; what is expected.

- There is careful time control. Starting on time and ending on time. Enough time is allowed to get the work done and no more.

- Committee members are sensitive to each other's needs and expressions. People listen and respect other's opinions.

- There is an informal, relaxed atmosphere, rather than a series of formal exchanges.

- There is good preparation by the staff person related to the committee, the committee chairperson and all committee members. Materials are well prepared and made available in advance in time for review and study. Everyone is appropriately prepared.

- Members are qualified and interested. A definite commitment exists.

- Interruptions are avoided or held to a minimum.

- Good minutes or records are kept so that agreements and decisions are not lost.

- Periodically the committee stops and assesses its own performance and works out necessary improvements.

- Recognition is provided and members feel they are really making a contribution.

- The work of the committee is given serious consideration, accepted and used, and makes a contribution to the work of the agency.

Indeed, committees can be effective if given proper leadership and attention. Some have said that the effectiveness of a board is measured by its committees, not the board itself; for it is at the committee level that a board will succeed or fail.

In Closing . . .

Getting the board of directors properly organized and fully functioning, as every board member and staff person knows, is very important. It's all to little avail, however, if the meetings of the board are not personally satisfying to members and productive in terms of moving the organization ahead. These matters are the focus of Chapter 8.

NOTES: Chapter 7

1. Bacon, Jeremy. "Corporate Directorship Practices." Quoted in *Harvard Business Review*, May-June, 1982, p. 30.

2. O'Connell, Brian. *Effective Leadership in Voluntary Organizations.* Walker and Company, 1981, pp. 71–72.

3. Weber, Joseph. *Managing the Board of Directors.* The Greater New York Fund, Inc., 1975, p. 4.

4. Trecker, Harleigh B. *Citizen Boards at Work.* Association Press, 1970.

5. Kuenzli, Gary. *Successful Board Leadership.* Management Resource Center YMCA's of Southern California, 1984, pp. 27–28.

6. Swanson, Andrew. *Building a Better Board: A Guide to Effective Leadership.* The Taft Group, 1984, p. 30.

7. Didactics Systems, Inc. *The Citizen Board in Voluntary Agencies.* United Way of America, 1979, p. 34.

8. Hardy, James M. *The Corporate Board in the YMCA.* YMCA of the USA, 1980, pp. 4–5.

chapter 8.

Conducting Productive and Satisfying Meetings

Although much of the business of nonprofit organizations is conducted in meetings, the majority of organizations spend little, if any, effort in making meetings productive and satisfying to participants. Research indicates that most board and committee members feel that meetings are too long, waste too much time and achieve nothing. If planned and conducted with thoughtfulness and common sense, however, it has been repeatedly demonstrated that meetings can create high attendance, improve the quality of decisions and promote alert follow-through.[1] The purpose of this chapter is to assist board chairs and chief executive officers in planning and conducting meetings that are exciting, stimulating, productive and satisfying.

123

Some Preliminaries for Success

There are a number of important factors which result in sustained, maximum board member attendance and production in meetings. Following are some standards for the preliminaries that contribute substantially to effective meetings:

- The setting must be attractive, comfortable and conducive to productive work. Assessability, convenient parking and good quality food service must be provided.

- Seating should encourage maximum participation. A large, round table, "hollow square" or circular seating in which members are facing the center encourage involvement of all. The "lecture" or "classroom" arrangement should be avoided.

- The meeting should be well planned and businesslike, but conducted in an atmosphere of warmth, informality and mature good humor.

- The agenda should always contain something of true significance—an important item that needs the board's consideration. If at least one such item is not on the docket, the meeting should be cancelled.

- The agenda, including all printed reports and reference materials, should be sent at least one week in advance of the meeting to all members for review and study.

- Meetings should start on time and not exceed the announced time of adjournment. Most board meetings can be conducted in a maximum of $1\frac{1}{2}$ hours unless exceptional issues or projects are being addressed.

124

- Occasionally meetings should be held in special settings. It might be in a branch building, program center or an affiliate's facility.

- Patterns and procedures of regular meetings should be reduced to routine as far as possible so that repetitive decisions do not have to be made. Such items as meeting time, place, frequency, some rules of practice, etc. should be regularized.

- Planned attention should be given to maximizing the involvement of all board members in discussion, review and decision making activities.

- Persons making reports should be alternated as much as possible and each should be given a specific time for presentation.

- An "RSVP" postcard should accompany the advanced agenda mailing and a reminder telephone call should be made to each member on either the day before or the day of the meeting.

The Board Agenda

Developing the board agenda is one of the most important functions that the board chair and the chief executive do together. The agenda should never be developed by only one party in isolation.

The best procedure that I have found for developing agendas is a face-to-face meeting approximately two weeks prior to the board meeting. In preparation, the chief executive should make a list of possible items for board consideration based on a review of past board minutes, reports and/or recommendations from committees of the board, emerging issues requiring board consideration and information items which

125

must be presented to the board for its edification. Additions and/or deletions should be made to the list during the meeting. At this point, the leaders must decide which of the items will be included on the next board agenda. As Joseph Weber points out, many organizations "load the agenda," thus creating a frustrating situation for the board in which the agenda is not completed within a specified time frame; or action items are rushed and not given sufficient board deliberation time.[2]

Prior to selecting specific agenda items, I have found that dividing the various agenda items into categories can be helpful. I use the following four categories:

1. **Information**—those items which do not require specific action by the board but are presented for the board's edification, background, knowledge and understanding. Information items are primarily reports (committees and staff), announcements or interpretive matters (i.e., program demonstrations). To the degree possible, information items should be printed and sent to the board in advance with the agenda. At the meeting, members can then discuss the matters and express opinions rather than simply listening to a bunch of verbal reports.[3]

2. **Action**—those items which require the board's approval and culminate in either board consensus or vote by the board.

3. **Review**—those items which require more discussion and consideration by the board than do the "information" items, but do not require approval. The product of the review may be increased understanding or advisement.

4. **Development**—those items which would benefit from receiving board input, ideas or suggestions—all without approval. This is a method of utilizing the board's resources to assist the staff and/or the board itself on matters which may subsequently be brought back to the board for information, review or action. Unfortunately,

this method is infrequently used in most boards, resulting in many board members feeling that their resources are underutilized.

In general, priority in selecting agenda items must be given to action items which require immediate decisions by the board versus those that might be considered at a later board meeting.

After the specific agenda items have been selected, consideration must be given to the format and flow of the meeting. Contrary to popular precedent, I do not think it necessary to follow a set order of business (i.e., minutes, treasurer's report, chief executive's report, committee reports, old business and new business). Variety in order and method is highly desirable and relieves the monotony of a set order. Usually, however, it is a good idea to have the items which appear on the agenda of every board meeting at the beginning of the meeting. These include: 1) approval of minutes (which have been sent in advance); 2) financial report; and 3) chief executive officer's report. It should be noted that a statement of the organization's current financial condition, including all income and expenditures for the month and year in relationship to budget, should be presented by the treasurer at *every* regular board meeting. The chief executive's report should be brief and occur at the beginning of the meeting because it will probably serve as an informational backdrop for consideration of subsequent agenda items.

In organizing the flow of the agenda, it is suggested that controversial issues and major action items be placed in the middle of the meeting or following the beginning items. It is never desirable to begin or to end a meeting with a controversial issue which might produce some negative feelings that can follow a heated discussion. If possible, conclude the meeting on an upbeat item or one in which board members can share a measure of pleasure or pride.[4]

Exhibit I is an example of a board meeting agenda of a hypothetical agency. It illustrates several previous points: inclusion of regular items, selectivity of agenda items, logical flow, and specification of actions

127

Exhibit I

AGENDA EXAMPLE
ANY AGENCY BOARD OF DIRECTORS MEETING

JOHN DOE, Board Chair, Presiding   September 15, 2001

<u>Expected Attendance</u>: Benson, Brown, Doe, Forrest, Gibbs, Gomez, Johnson, Lewis, Meir, Mitchell, Richardson, Small, Smith, Thompson, Thomas, Van, Vernon, Walker, Wilson, Zane. <u>Staff</u>: Jones, Wharton. <u>Expected Absences</u>: Black, Cook, Daniel, Foster, Wright.

1. <u>MEETING CALLED TO ORDER / INVOCATION</u> . . . . .JOHN DOE
   (Board Chair)

2. <u>REPORT OF CHIEF EXECUTIVE OFFICER</u> (*Information* — Exhibit A) . . . .
   . . . . MARY JONES
   (Chief Executive)

3. <u>APPROVAL OF MINUTES OF AUGUST 15 MEETING</u> (*Action* — Exhibit B) . . . . .
   . . . . .TOM SMITH
   (Secretary)

4. <u>FINANCIAL COMMITTEE REPORT</u> . . . . BOB BROWN
   (Treasurer)

   — Preliminary budget for next year (*Review*, action next month — Exhibit C)

   — August Financial Statements (*Action* — Exhibits D and E)

5. <u>CURRENT SUPPORT CAMPAIGN COMMITTEE REPORT</u> . . . . . . HENRY LEWIS
   (Committee Chair)

   — Next year's campaign goal (*Action* — Exhibit F)

   — Theme ideas and activities for campaign (*Development*)

6. <u>PURCHASE OF DAY CAMP SITE</u> . . . . .JOHN DOE
   (Chair Board/Executive Committee)

   — Recommendations of Executive Committee (*Action* — Exhibit G)

7. <u>PROGRAM COMMITTEE REPORT</u> (*Information*) . . . . SUE GIBBS
   (Committee Chair)

   — Statistical report (Exhibit H)

8. OTHER MATTERS

9. NEXT MEETING: OCTOBER 16

10. ADJOURN

to be taken (category). In addition, Exhibit I illustrates the desirability of: indicating expected attendance and absences—a permanent record but also a subtle reminder of the importance of meeting attendance; listing of names opposite topics (not the title in parenthesis which is for reader identification only)—this specifies the responsibility and informs the board who will present the topic; spreading of presentational responsibility; providing opportunity for other agenda items of importance; calling attention to next meeting.[5]

Maximizing Board Member Participation

The positive effects of participation on productivity in organizational functioning have been recognized for some time through definitive research.[6] Although there are reams of data and scores of volumes which attest to the efficacy of participation—involving people in the organization's work so that they can have a sense of ownership—fewer than twenty percent of today's managers accept the idea.[7] From discussions with several board chairs, my hunch is that many do not view the use of participatory techniques as being "businesslike." Indeed, many view participation as a waste of valuable time. In light of this situation, it is ironic that nearly one half of corporate executives who serve on nonprofit boards feel that they are underutilized.[8] The positive results of participation and the outcry of board members to be involved cannot be ignored. Board chairs and chief executives must take the lead in creating opportunities for board members to participate, to be involved and to provide help. Toward this end, the following methods of involvement are offered:

● **Board Chair as Discussion Leader**—It can be very helpful for the board chair to see him/herself as a discussion leader on agenda items where participation is needed. Here are some suggestions from Cyril R. Mill that might be helpful: [9]

—When someone is speaking, look more to other members of the board than at the speaker. This helps encourage interaction among board members.

—Do not make a reply to each comment by a member. Wait for someone else to do so. If necessary, ask the group, "Any reaction to that?"

—If someone talks overly long, interrupt by saying, "I'm losing the point you are making. Can you state it for me very briefly?"

—When questions are directed toward the chair, if appropriate, refer them back to the group: "Someone here must have a response to that."

—If you think you have grasped a complex point someone has tried to express, clarify it for the board by saying, "Let's see, if I understand you, you are saying . . ."

—Avoid making personal comments that may be taken as disapproval, condescension, sarcasm, personal cross-examination or self-approval.

—Summarize periodically.

—Do not insist on having the last word.

● **Shared Leadership**—There are a variety of functions and activities to be performed in a board meeting and all of these should not be performed by the board chair. Indeed, responsibilities for specific activities before, during and following board meetings should be delegated as much as possible to board members and, as previously noted, presentation responsibilities should be rotated among members rather than always falling to the same few persons. Correspondingly, staff participation in board meetings should be minimized with contributions being limited to providing technical or resource information pertinent to the board's deliberations or providing background information related to specific agenda items.

● **The Gatekeeping Function**—In terms of techniques of involvement, probably no other group function is as significant as that of gatekeeping. Simply stated, gatekeeping is the function of helping all members get into the board's discussions. Some theorists say it is the responsibility of all members to operationalize the gatekeeping function, but I find that a bit impractical. Initially, performing the gatekeeping function must be the responsibility of the board chair and the chief executive. When effectively performing the function, the gatekeeper opens up communication channels by encouraging or facilitating participation of others or by proposing standards for regulating the flow of communication so that everyone has a chance to contribute. Although most people intuitively recognize that it is important to listen to the ideas and opinions of others in reaching decisions, they are not always aware that it is sometimes necessary to "open the gate" for other members so that their ideas and opinions may be expressed. For example, simply ask the silent member a question like, "Jim, you've been in a number of similar situations, what do you think about this matter?" Another way to "open gates" is for the board chair to "go around the table" asking each person in turn to briefly state where they are on the issue under discussion. Gatekeeping can be performed in relatively simple ways, but with a very profound result.

● **Sub-Groups**—For some agenda items at a board meeting, it helps to divide into sub-groups—particularly for those agenda items in the "development" and "review" categories. Sub-groups keep people more involved in the meeting by giving each person an opportunity for more "air time." Sub-grouping can also be a fast way to complete some tasks. The purpose of sub-groups is to generate inputs, suggestions, ideas and/or proposals for consideration of the total board or the staff. Sub-groups should never be charged with making major decisions. To be effective, sub-groups should be: 1) small (5–7 persons); 2) well instructed in terms of task, expectations, guidance, etc.; 3) assigned a short work time (i.e., 15 minutes); 4) prepared to report using flip chart or other visual aids. Time should be scheduled on the agenda for all groups to report and to discuss any revisions or reactions and move, if required, to decision.[10]

● **Brainstorming**—This is a technique that is useful when divergent thinking is needed in a meeting in order to generate a lot of ideas. It equalizes participation, encourages creativity and adds excitement and variety to meetings. Brainstorming usually takes from five to twenty minutes and it can be conducted in small groups (five to seven persons) or in the total board on a "round robin" or free-for-all basis. Prior to beginning, it is important to make the subject being brainstormed very clear. The following rules for brainstorming should be presented prior to beginning:

—No discussion or evaluation of an idea is allowed.

—Volume counts—the more the better.

—All ideas recorded.

—Building on ideas of others is encouraged.

—Afterwards, all ideas will be evaluated and the most useful will be tested.

Board Roles

When a board meets it can expect to have both *task* and *maintenance* functions. In other words, some of the essential roles in a board are

132

task related in that they help the board to accomplish things, and some are maintenance roles in that they contribute to strengthening and maintaining group life. Both task and maintenance roles have been determined to be necessary for a smoothly functioning and effective group.[11] These roles may be assumed by separate board members or shared by various members at different points in meetings and, in many cases, one or more individual members may fulfill more than one role. Although board members fulfill the roles in various combinations, it can be very instructive for board chairs and chief executives to be familiar with all roles.

Task Roles

- **Initiator** . . proposes tasks or actions; defines group problems; suggests ways to proceed, ideas for solving a problem or ways to tackle a task.

- **Information Seeker** . . asks for clarification of facts and opinions; requests facts, opinions, ideas and feelings pertinent to the discussion.

- **Informer** . . offers facts or generalizations; provides relevant information.

- **Clarifier** . . interprets ideas or suggestions; clears up confusion; defines terms; clarifies issues.

- **Summarizer** . . pulls together related ideas; restates suggestions.

- **Reality Tester** . . makes critical analysis of ideas; tests ideas against data to see if ideas will work.

- **Consensus Tester** . . asks if group is nearing a decision; offers decisions or conclusions for group to accept or reject.

133

Maintenance Roles

- **Harmonizer** . . attempts to reconcile disagreements; reduces tension; gets people to explore differences.

- **Gatekeeper** . . helps get others into the discussion; suggests procedures that facilitate sharing by all members.

- **Encourager** . . is warm, friendly and responsive to others; communicates acceptance of others' contributions; offers praise and support to others.

- **Compromiser** . . modifies position in interest of group cohesion or growth; admits errors; offers compromises that yield status when his or her own ideas are involved in conflicts.

- **Standard Setter** . . points out explicit or implicit norms that have been set; suggests procedures; tests group's satisfaction with its procedures.

Use of Roles—With the leadership of the board chair and the chief executive, it can be useful for a board to determine which roles, both task and maintenance, are fulfilled by which members. If certain roles are absent, members can plan to incorporate the associated behaviors into their own functioning in the board. In addition, determining roles allows members to form a clear perception of their value to the board and they can consciously extend the behaviors that they naturally exhibit and that are comfortable to them. This kind of utilization of members' resources provides for shared leadership in the board and stimulates creativity, higher group morale, interest and concern.

In Conclusion . . .

Board meetings should be productive for the organization and exciting and stimulating for members of the board. Board meetings should also be occasions for decision making—the subject of our next chapter.

NOTES: *Chapter 8*

1. O'Connell, Brian. *Conducting Good Meetings*. Independent Sector, 1988, p. 3.

2. Weber, Joseph. *Managing the Board of Directors*. The Greater New York Fund, Inc., 1975, pp. 19–20.

3. Poummit, Morris R. "Are Your Board Meetings Bored Meetings?" *Nonprofit World*, 1988, p. 11.

4. Swanson, Andrew. *Building a Better Board*. The Taft Group, 1984, p. 17.

5. Sorenson, Roy. *The Art of Board Membership*. Association Press, 1953, pp. 73–76.

6. Marrow, A. J., D. G. Bower and S. E. Seashore. *Management by Participation*. Harper and Row, 1967.

7. Hall, Jay. *Ponderables*. Teleometrics International, 1982, p. 13.

8. Fenn, Dan H., Jr. "Executives As Community Leaders." *Harvard Business Review*, March–April, 1971.

9. Mill, Cyril R. *Activities for Trainers*. Quoted in *Successful Board Leadership*. Management Resource Center YMCA's of Southern California, 1984, pp. 25–26.

10. Eberhardt, Louise. "Holding Productive and Satisfying Board Meetings." *The Nonprofit Board Book*. Independent Community Consultants, 1985, p. 42.

11. Bradford, Leland P. *Making Meetings Work*. University Associates, 1976, pp. 35–46.

chapter 9.

Decision Making in Boards and Committees

———————————————

Many boards of directors make limited, if any, use of systematic analysis in decision making. Typically, there is heavy reliance on staff or committee recommendations with an implicit assumption that analytical thinking has been applied. Such reliance substantially reduces the board's direct involvement in decision making. In many cases, this reliance on staff and committees is both understandable and justified. For decisions of major importance to the organization, however, much more analysis and commitment is necessary if the organization is to have high quality decisions and the support needed for implementation. Longitudinal research indicates a strong positive relationship between the degree to which one participates in making board decisions and his or her subsequent level of commitment to both the decision and the organization.[1] Certainly more analytical thinking is desirable for board decision making, but real involvement on the part of all board members is absolutely necessary for major decisions. The purpose of this chapter is to assist board chairs and chief executives

136

in increasing analytical thinking and broadening the base of involvement in board and committee decision making.

Robert's Rules

In making group decisions, most boards use Robert's Rules of Order as a standard procedure. Certainly General Henry M. Robert, the author of "Robert's Rules," and his successors in the parliamentary field have made several important contributions: provided an authoritative set of rules to follow and made boards aware of the need for orderly procedure in conducting business. Initially, Robert's Rules were developed for large parliamentary bodies. Used in smaller, modern boards of directors, the rigid application of parliamentary procedure has created the following kinds of problems: [2]

1. The unbending adherence to the rules has made group process excessively arbitrary and monotonous.

2. Strict adherence to the rules has injected an icy formality into discussions which has hampered the development of a warm, friendly atmosphere. In many cases, the free and easy exchange of ideas and feelings is hampered and group productivity is stifled.

3. The rule that discussions must take place only after a motion places the "cart before the horse" in that a solution or a decision is proposed before all of the facts and alternatives are known.

4. Voting encourages winning and losing and it can be very divisive. Some say that even ranking is often desirable to voting because group members can reflect a range of choices.[3] In using voting, it must be remembered that a 51 percent majority vote is not a group decision, for almost half of the group is against the proposal. This does not mean

137

that there are no occasions when a board should vote on an issue. For many boards, in many situations, however, formulating a statement of consensus is preferable.

Consensus Decision Making

Consensus means that every member of a group, be it a board or committee, has an opportunity to influence the final decision. Members of the group reach substantial agreement, not necessarily unanimity. In seeking consensus, members strive for a decision which is best for all and which all members regard as fair.

As noted previously, group action requires group decision, not a majority vote. Consensus is the best way that I know of for developing group decisions and contributing to group cohesion, while motions and voting increase the risk of group divisiveness. Simply by building a decision together through give and take discussion and genuine listening, differences of opinion are narrowed and agreement is reached. In addition, opinions often change in light of new facts and information, particularly if persons are not forced to defend their original ideas but rather are free to change their minds without embarrassment or apology.

Obtaining consensus in boards and committees is harder work than formalistic modes of decision making, but the investment of time and energy can have a dramatic payoff. Here are some guidelines for board and committee members, in part from the research of Jay Hall, that can be shared with groups that are working to achieve consensus.[4]

1. **Avoid arguing for your own position.** Present it as lucidly and logically as possible, but be sensitive to and consider seriously the reactions of the group in any subsequent presentation of the same point.

138

2. **Avoid "win-lose" statements in the discussion of opinions.** Discard the notion that someone must win and someone must lose in the discussion. When impasses occur, look for the next most acceptable alternative for all parties involved.

3. **Avoid changing your mind only in order to side-step conflict and to reach agreement and harmony.** Withstand pressures to yield which have no objective or logical foundation.

4. **Avoid conflict-reducing techniques such as majority vote, averaging, bargaining, coin-flipping, "horse trading,"** etc. Treat differences of opinion as indicative of incomplete sharing of relevant information on someone's part.

5. **View differences of opinion as both natural and helpful rather than as a hindrance in decision making.** Generally, the expression of ideas and opinions increases the array and richness of resources which can be used by the group.

6. **Avoid subtle forms of influence and decision modification.** For example, when a dissenting member finally agrees, don't feel that he or she must be "rewarded" by having his or her own way on a subsequent point.

7. **Accept responsibility for both hearing and being heard.** Strive to include all members in what is decided and always listen intensely for meaning and understanding.

8. **Be willing to entertain the possibility that your group can achieve all of the above and actually excel at its job and tasks.** Avoid doomsaying ("consensus won't work—let's vote"); negative predictions of group potential ("This group can't agree on anything—let's vote"); or a return to the easy and comfortable ways of making decisions ("It's getting late—let's vote").

Two cautions are in order when using consensus decision making. First, be sure that the use of consensus is genuine. Anne Spenser has found that when ties among some board members become exclusionary, decisions may look as if they are being made by consensus when in fact they have been made by an inner core. In this sense, consensus decision making is used as a protective device to maintain the power of the more influential members.[5] Board members know when they are being manipulated—when their time is being wasted and when the activities that they are involved in are useless. Leaders must make consensus real and genuine or be prepared to suffer a considerable backlash. Second, consensus is *not* a process of compromise—the integrity of all members must be constantly protected while seeking consensus. Some of the desired behaviors delineated in the above guidelines may, in the perception of some, come perilously close to a compromise process. To the contrary, however, these are the behaviors that are necessary to achieve an unfreezing of rigidly held positions which are usually major barriers to group decision making. While working toward an objective of *all* members being in substantial agreement renders compromise a remote possibility, care must always be exercised by leadership to ensure that the group does not run roughshod over any of its members.

I have used consensus decision making with literally hundreds of different decision groups. In all cases the decisions have been very important and in some cases, the decisions were highly charged emotionally. The groups have varied in size from relatively small boards and committees to very large planning conferences. All of these groups, except one, have arrived at consensus. In some cases it appeared that consensus was not possible but through the commitment and work of people of good will, it was achieved. When members strive for what is best for all rather than trying to triumph over opponents, they ensure organizational success and they also fulfill the highest expectations of the democratic tradition.

Decision Analysis: Concepts of Analytical Thinking

Some board chairs, chief executives, board committees and entire boards have found the basic concepts of analytical thinking to be helpful in decision making. When combined with a lot of common sense, analytical thinking can help a group make the best use of limited time and available information. The essence of these concepts is contained in the four basic imperatives for analysis in decision making.[6]

1. **Think Analytically.** Time spent on a decision problem is divided between two basic tasks: gathering and processing information, and thinking. The evidence indicates that most people devote about 99 percent of their decision making time to gathering and processing information—talking to people about the issue, reading material, retrieving data, developing complex models or theories and carrying out elaborate calculations. Although these activities may be useful, it is usually true that a more intelligent decision can be reached by spending more time in hard thinking—trying to pin down the essence of the issue, key criteria and viable options. The difficulty with much analysis is that it is so complex that its relationship to the problem to be solved is obscure. Complexity notwithstanding, however, more energy and time generally needs to be devoted to thinking intelligently about the problem at hand. Often such thinking requires the ability to use simple numbers and understand their implications. Richard Zeckhauser of Harvard argues that "one of the best tools of policy analysis is long division because it's the simplest method for answering the question, 'How much did I accomplish for how much?' Thinking analytically about most decisions involves an ability to handle simple numbers or what has been called 'a fluency in the elementary language of mathematics.'"

2. **Break It Down.** To analyze a problem involves decomposing it—breaking it down into its component parts. The process of decomposition involves: breaking the decision into its most important com-

141

ponents; working individually with the components; and recombining the results to make the decision. Unfortunately most people are reluctant to decompose problems on a conscious and systematic basis. Apparently, they are confident that their minds can make consistent and intelligent choices every time. Unfortunately, research in cognitive psychology is proving the opposite. George A. Miller of Harvard started it when he discovered "the magical number of seven, plus or minus two"—that is, the inability of the human mind to hold more than five to nine bits of information in short-term memory. There are limits to human rationality, but they can be overcome by breaking decisions down into component parts.

3. **Make It Simple.** Most important decisions are so complicated that it is impossible to analyze them completely. For example, to undertake a complete analysis, one would be required to: specify all possible decision alternatives; predict all possible consequences of every alternative; estimate the probability of every consequence; appraise the desirability of every consequence; and calculate which decision alternative yields the most desirable set of circumstances. Such an ideal and rational approach cannot be attained in most organizations because of the limits of time, information and intellectual capacity. Essentially, if any decision problem is to be resolved in a limited amount of time, it is impossible to take into account all of the possibly relevant factors. It must be simplified and, in all probability, simplified drastically.

For most people, the logic of simplification is a difficult concept. Everyone feels uncomfortable leaving things out. Moreover, the idea of simplification carries some unfortunate perceptions, namely that for one to do simplified analysis implies simplistic thinking that is unworthy of the human mind. Apparently many are unaware of the vast difference between what is simple and what is simplistic. Consequently, the tendency is to use as many factors as possible in the time available. Regardless of how many factors are used, the choice will inevitably be based on very few factors, perhaps only one or two.

142

In using analytical simplification, it should be kept in mind that: 1) People can consider only a limited number of factors. Consequently, it only makes sense to select explicitly and carefully those few on which to concentrate; 2) Simplified analysis can be based on the decision maker's conscious judgments about which factors are important and which are not; 3) Simplification works in large part because it encourages decision makers to use intuition to its best advantage. Simplification provides a clear structure for making intuitive but explicit judgments about each of the important factors and concentrates the decision maker's intuition where it will make a difference. Care should be exercised, however, to be certain that intuition is not used to the exclusion of systematic, step-by-step procedures. A preference on the part of decision makers to rely solely on intuition and judgment can lead to serious distortions of reality and produce decision debacles.[7]

As stated by Behn and Vaupel, "The question is not whether to simplify; any decision maker must—and will. The only question is whether this process of simplification will be unconscious or conscious, disorganized or analytical."[8]

4. **Specify.** Decisions depend upon judgments—judgments about the factors used in a decisional situation and their relative importance, the options to be considered, the probabilities of events, etc. Decision making is inherently subjective, but that does not mean that it should be vague. Neither does it mean that decisions should not be objectified to the extent possible. As slippery and impossible as complete objectivity may be, we should proceed in its direction. For example, it is very important to identify the major factors that will be used in a decision situation and to make them as specific and clear as possible. These factors (or criteria or values) that are important in assessing all options should each have data indicators. Data indicators specify the kinds of data or information needed to determine the degree to which all factors are impacted by each option. In order to make valid judgments, decision makers will need as high a degree of specification as possible in the data indicators. To achieve the desired level

143

of specification, data indicators should either: 1) be quantified (e.g., trends, percentages, ratios, etc.); or 2) describe conditions that will exist when the factor has been fulfilled; or 3) indicate satisfactory quality levels to be attained in fulfilling the factor.

It should be noted that in striving for specification, "quantitative" decision makers can let their technical capacities be a substitute for their own judgments. Decisions should be based upon those factors that the decision makers believe to be most important, not upon ones for which quantified data can be found. Even when quantification is not appropriate or possible, it is important to attain a high degree of specificity in the data indicators.

In sum, the thoughtful use of systematic analysis can improve decision making in boards and committees. It is abundantly clear from a decade or more of research, however, that the human mind needs tools. A description of such a tool follows. This tool, a decision matrix, is an example of how the concepts of analytical thinking can be incorporated into a practical tool to support decision making.

The Decision Matrix: An Analytic Tool for Decision Makers

Exhibit I is a decision matrix that can be used in many different kinds of decision situations.[9] The reader will note that the matrix and instructions are quite similar to those used in Chapter 4, but the context is substantially different. The matrix has been extensively tested with boards and committees of various sized organizations in a variety of decisional situations. The matrix is very flexible in that it can be used in small and large groups and on an individual basis. It can be used exceptionally well by board committees and special task forces and, for major decisions, by the entire board of directors. The decision

Exhibit I
DECISION MATRIX

CRITERIA	IMPORTANCE WEIGHT	OPTION 1:	OPTION 2:	OPTION 3:	OPTION 4:
TOTALS:					

matrix is similar to a relatively new technique, Multiattribute Utility Analysis, but it is considerably more flexible and useable.[10]

A very important precursor in using the decision matrix is determining the five most important criteria or factors to be used in making judgments about each of the options. In keeping with the prior discussion of analytical concepts, it is recommended that not more than five key criteria be used. Here are some examples of criteria from a nonprofit organization whose board had to make a decision regarding the priority of capital projects which would be financed among ten branch operations:

> —Evidence of past and potential ability of branch to raise necessary annual operating income, both earned and subsidy income.

> —Evidence of strong board and volunteer involvement.

> —Direct impact of branch project on the total organization's goals, strategies and future plans.

Experience indicates that the criteria used in major organizational decisions should be:

- **Testable**—In other words, each criterion should be such that evidence (data indicators) can be provided which will serve as a basis for making a judgment concerning the degree to which the criterion is or can be fulfilled. This does *not* mean that only criteria for which quantification can be provided should be selected. As previously noted, data indicators can specify conditions and/or quality levels desired in lieu of quantification.

- **Mutually Exclusive**—Each criterion should, to the greatest possible degree, stand on its own and not overlap with another criterion.

146

- **Clear and Terse**—Each criterion statement should be understandable and as briefly stated as possible. Extended statements or compounded sentences tend to confuse more than enlighten.

- **Limited in Number**—It is suggested that not more than five criteria be used. Research indicates that most major organizational decisions are made on the basis of five or less criteria. To develop an extended list of criteria unnecessarily complicates the decision process.

After the key criteria have been selected, data indicators need to be developed for each criterion. In the example used previously, one of the criteria selected was: "Evidence of past and potential ability of branch to raise necessary annual operating income, both earned and subsidy income." The data indicators which were developed for this criterion were: 1) Net financial operating position for past three years; 2) Income from membership and program fees for past three years; 3) Sustaining membership income (contributions) for past three years; 4) Three-year pro forma operating statement, assuming proposed facilities.

Following the specification of data indicators, all data needed are retrieved and placed in a data booklet for use in making the decision.

The work session for decision making is the culminating event in using the decision matrix. The attendance and time for the work session will vary in accord with the particular decisional situation. If the decision is a recommendation to be made by a committee, the attendance may be small and the time relatively short. On the other hand, if the decision is to be made by the board, it will involve a larger group and more time. In the example of the capital priorities work session, the group was large (45 persons) because of the need for the board to be involved along with key leadership from all branches. That meeting lasted approximately five hours, but it affected the organization's future for the next ten years.

147

Exhibit II contains the instructions for completing the decision matrix. When the matrix is used in a group, the rankings and ratings for each option on each criterion should be done by consensus, using the previously delineated guidelines. This will not only improve the quality of the decision, but the involvement will result in increased ownership, commitment and support for implementation.

Decision Making Sequence

There are many decision models or problem solving processes available to groups. The one I like most is detailed in Exhibit III. It consists of ten decision making steps that I have found to be especially useful for boards, board committees and task forces.

Many times the kinds of decisions that face a board will not be of the magnitude and importance that requires the use of the decision matrix and its attendant process. In those cases, the decision making sequence delineated in Exhibit III can be very helpful. In implementing the sequence, a consensus style of decision making, as previously discussed, should again be used at all points. Consensus seeking will make the implementation of all decision making steps more difficult. The results, however, will make the effort more than worthwhile.

In Conclusion . . .

At times board decision making can be frustrating, confusing and exhausting. At other times it can be stimulating, enjoyable and exciting. Unavoidably, however, the board is charged with the responsibility of

Exhibit II

INSTRUCTIONS: DECISION MATRIX

Step 1: List all <u>criteria</u> that are important in this decision. Choose the five most important criteria from the list and write each in a separate box in column 1, "Criteria." Now decide which of the criteria is most important and place a "10" opposite that criterion in column 2, "Importance." Compare the other four criteria to the first choice and assign each an appropriate number from 1 – 9. Ask such questions as, "Is this criterion about 80% as important as the first criterion?" If so, assign the criterion an importance weight of 8. Continue until all criteria have a relative importance weight in column 2.

Step 2: Write the four most viable decision options in columns 3 through 6. Compare each of the four options against each of the criteria listed. Assign a rating of 10 to the option that best satisfies the particular criterion under consideration. Rate the other options relative to the best—rating them less than 10 as appropriate. Place the ratings in the upper left hand corner of each box. Continue until all options have been rated for each criterion.

Step 3: Multiply the importance weight of each criterion by the rating of the option against that criterion and enter the resulting number in the small box. An example:

Rating of Option Against Criterion   8   40   Importance Weight X Rating of Option

Add the numbers in the small boxes and enter total on bottom line for each option.

IMPORTANT: This procedure provides a comparative analysis of how well each decision option satisfies the important criteria. The procedure does not make the decision—there will probably be other factors that need to be considered in making the decision and other people that need to be involved. However, this procedure can provide meaningful insights and assistance in making the decision.

Exhibit III

DECISION MAKING STEPS

1. STATE THE PROBLEM CLEARLY.

   Be sure enough information is available so that the real problem is stated rather than a symptom or just part of the problem.

2. DEFINE THE ESSENTIAL CRITERIA A SOLUTION MUST MEET TO BE SATISFACTORY.

   Then list any other conditions to be fulfilled which would be desirable, if feasible.

3. USE BRAINSTORMING TO SEARCH FOR SOLUTIONS – LIST THEM.

   Try to use different frames of reference and perspectives to develop creative solutions.

4. OBTAIN ALL THE FACTS RELEVANT TO EACH PROPOSED SOLUTION AND RELATE THEM TO THE ESSENTIAL CRITERIA.

5. EVALUATE THE SOLUTIONS TO DETERMINE THE EXTENT TO WHICH THEY MEET THE ESSENTIAL CRITERIA.

   Check to be sure the solution does not produce unacceptable side effects.

6. DECIDE ON THE SOLUTION WHICH BEST MEETS THE ESSENTIAL CRITERIA.

7. CHECK THE SOLUTION FINALLY SELECTED AGAINST THE PROBLEM AS STATED.

   Be sure the solution really solves the problem.

8. SPECIFY THE ACTION PLAN FOR IMPLEMENTING THE DECISION.

   Who? What? How? By when?

9. SPECIFY AN ACTION PLAN FOR ASSESSING HOW WELL THE DECISION IS BEING IMPLEMENTED.

   What information is required to make this assessment? Who will collect it? How? Who will make the assessment and report success achieved to the group?

10. IMPLEMENT THE DECISION.

making major decisions that will ultimately determine the agency's future. Increasing analytical thinking and involvement of the board and its committees in decision making will be a major step in ensuring excellence in that future.

NOTES: *Chapter 9*

1. Hall, Jay. *Toward Group Effectiveness*. Teleometrics International, 1971, p. 2.

2. Lowry, Sheldon G. and John S. Holik. *A New Look at Parliamentary Procedure*. North Central Regional Extension Publications, 1985, p. 1.

3. Moore, Carl M. *Group Techniques for Idea Building*. Sage Publications, 1987, p. 136.

4. Hall, op. cit., p. 8.

5. Middleton, Melissa. "Nonprofit Boards of Directors: Beyond the Governance Function." *The Nonprofit Sector* edited by Walter W. Powell, Yale University Press, 1987, p. 149.

6. Behn, Robert D. and James W. Vaupel. *Quick Analysis for Busy Decision Makers*. Basic Books, Inc., 1982, pp. 16–23.

7. Nutt, Paul C. *Making Tough Decisions*. Jossey-Bass Publishers, 1989, p. 30.

8. Behn and Vaupel, op. cit., p. 20.

9. Hardy, James M. "Individual Values." *Managing Individual Development Program*, JMH Associates, 1980, pp. 13–15.

10. Ulvila, Jacob W. and Rex V. Brown. "Decision Analysis Comes of Age." *Harvard Business Review*, September–October, 1982, pp. 136–140.

chapter 10.

Recognizing Board Members

This is going to be the shortest chapter in this book, but it's not because the subject is unimportant. Indeed, providing genuine and well deserved recognition to board members for their multiple contributions is one of the most important and frequently neglected components of board development. I find it difficult and somewhat frustrating to write about recognition in a way that is specific and useful, but just as importantly, in a way that avoids reiterating the obvious and underscoring the trite. But that has not stopped me from trying. Consequently, the purpose of this chapter is to assist agency leadership in becoming increasingly sensitive to the need for recognition and to provide guidance and assistance that fulfills this need.

Some Principles of Board Recognition

● **Recognition needs to be personalized and creatively appropriate to individuals.** It takes time and thought to plan recognition that is special and individualized, but it's worth it. The board chair of one of my client organizations had made an enormous contribution to the organization by serving during three critical years of the organization's development. The entire board and the chief executive wanted to give him something in recognition of his immense contribution, but the man was wealthy and generally "had everything." He loved horses and loved to ride and by careful listening, the chief executive and an officer of the board found out that his favorite saddle was greatly deteriorated after years of wear, but that he would not purchase a new saddle because as he said, "It fits like an old shoe." During one of the chairman's extended trips, the officers took the old saddle to a fine saddlemaker for complete measurement and returned the saddle unobserved to his ranch. A new, beautiful saddle was made which was an exact fit and an engraved plate, with an appropriate expression of appreciation from the organization, was actually made into the back of the saddle. Needless to say, the honoree was overcome when the saddle was presented at the organization's annual meeting. It's interesting to note too that he now serves as chair of the organization's board of governors—an advisory and fund raising group composed of very prominent people who want to continuously support the organization. Undoubtedly, the creative and highly personalized recognition he received was a major factor in his continuing to serve the organization at a new and significant level.

● **Recognition is a process rather than a product; a becoming, rather than an ending.**[1] Recognition should be creative, continuous and diverse. Although there are some parts of an agency's recognition program that can be standardized, recognition cannot be totally prepackaged.

● **Recognition should be genuine and timely.** It is neither necessary nor desirable to wait until people retire from the board or even

153

until the annual meeting to provide encouragement and recognition. Many times this can be done on a one-to-one basis when a significant contribution has been made. It's even more meaningful if it can be done in front of the entire board.

● **Recognition must strike the delicate balance.** Some organizations give too many awards to too many people. The effect is a diluting of the importance of service. Efforts should be made to provide enough so that everyone is justly recognized for work well done, but not too much to cause the recognition to lose value and meaning.

● **Recognition should not only include those in the limelight but also those who stay in the background and make things happen.** Many times only those who are outfront and in visible leadership positions gather the kudos. Care must be exercised to also recognize those loyal and dedicated persons who consistently make major contributions behind the scenes and those who "stay the course and occupy the trenches."

● **Recognition should take a variety of forms.** Recognition can be: formal and informal; spontaneous and planned; one-to-one and in groups; involve tangible gifts and verbal expression; etc. If recognition is well deserved, genuine and personalized, almost any form is appreciated. This includes, of course, the much maligned presentation of pins, plaques, badges, scrolls and certificates. These are important and mean a great deal to people and agencies should not be afraid to spend some money on them.[2] I'm consistently impressed with how much recognition gifts and mementos mean to people and how they are displayed in homes and offices with great pride.

Some Recognition Ideas

At a very basic level, recognition is simply the application of thoughtfulness as an expression of appreciation for the contributions which a person has made. Consequently, the forms of recognition are literally unlimited. In general, recognition is most meaningful if done in the presence of those who are most important to the honoree (i.e., family, close friends, peers, etc.). For some people, it may also be important to make the recognition as broad-based as possible by, for example, the use of media. Effective recognition, however, ranges from simple one-to-one acts to more complex and involved events and activities. Following are some possibilities for use by board chairs and chief executives that span this range.[3,4,5] Hopefully these will stimulate other ideas and adaptations on the part of the reader.

- Unexpected notes or telephone calls expressing thanks.

- Praising persons to their families and friends (it will get back to them).

- Letters to family members praising the person's contributions and thanking them for sharing the person.

- Small mementos, gifts or cards at special times of year.

- Job rotation opportunities that broaden experience and learning.

- Job assignments that offer increased responsibility and authority.

- Job assignments that provide opportunities for interaction with highest authorities.

- Opportunities to meet and work with people of influence.

- Tapes of a person's speeches.

- Opportunity to have name connected to something in writing (i.e., book, article, etc.).

155

- Letters of commendation for specific achievement to the person's paid boss or board chair.

- Letters of commendation for important achievements and contributions to editors of town, area, college, hometown, fraternal, professional, service or church newspapers and magazines.

- Story in newsletters telling of person's impact on people and/or programs.

- Opportunities to participate in workshops, conferences and conventions.

- Nomination in area, state or national recognition programs and/or for positions.

- Tangible awards noting service: plaques, pins, badges or certificates that can be displayed.

- Special tribute at annual meeting or large public gathering or event held in honor of person.

- Award named for person: for people-related accomplishments (humanitarian, nurturing, etc.) or for influential achievements.

- On-going program, site or facility named for person.

Desired Recognition

A recent study of 145 board and committee members addressed the types of recognition desired by volunteers.[6] Seventy-two of the 145 respondents checked "one-to-one recognition by the board or committee chair" as the type of recognition desired; thirty-eight checked "media publicity;" thirty-three checked "circulation of a membership roster among volunteers and companies;" thirty-two checked "promotions to higher leadership levels;" and thirty-one checked "certificates." Although a few indicated other responses, the above five items constituted the major types of recognition desired by the respondents.

There is little mention in the literature of the desire for recognition and status on the part of board members. However, these motives should not be overlooked by board chairs and chief executives. Auerbach states that, "the coin of the realm . . . is recognition, prestige and status." In his opinion, there is never too much of it and the danger is that rather too little may be bestowed, thus bringing about indifference or even hostility on the part of board members.[7]

In Closing . . .

Everyone likes to have his or her efforts recognized—it's a natural and pervasive need. There is no basic contradiction between the normal desire for recognition and dedicated devotion to the work of an agency. Board chairs and chief executives can substantially increase board members' motivation and contributions by providing personalized, creative, genuine and timely recognition. Providing recognition takes both time and effort, but most of all it takes a very large measure of human sensitivity and thoughtfulness.

NOTES: Chapter 10

1. Vineyard, Sue. *Beyond Banquets, Plaques and Pens: Creative Ways to Recognize Volunteers and Staff.* Heritage Arts, 1981, pp. 3–4.

2. O'Connell, Brian. *Finding, Developing and Rewarding Good Board Members.* Independent Sector, 1988, p. 13.

3. Munson, Mary K. *Creative Recognition Ideas* (Appendix G). University of Illinois 4-H Youth, 1987.

4. Gates, Virginia E., editor. *Helping Hands.* YMCA of Metropolitan Chicago, 1979, pp. 127–128.

5. Educational Services Unit. *Volunteer Resource Book.* Girl Scouts of the U.S.A., 1982, p. 20.

6. Schoderbek, Peter P. *The Board and Its Responsibilities.* United Way of America, 1983, pp. 3–4.

7. Auerbach, Arnold. Quoted by Peter P. Schoderbek in *The Board and Its Responsibilities.* United Way of America, 1983, p. 4.

chapter 11.

Evaluating Boards

As noted in prior chapters, there is growing evidence that the quality of board performance has a great bearing on the quality of programs and services provided by the organization. Essentially, when there is an effective board, there is a far better chance that the organization's programs and services will be good. Because of this great responsibility to their communities and the larger society, boards must guarantee to themselves, as well as to the people they serve, that they are doing the best job possible. Indeed, they must look at their own work more carefully and devote more time to systematic evaluation of their efforts. The purpose of this chapter is to assist board chairs and chief executives in giving leadership to evaluating the efficacy of their board of directors as a basis for continuous board development.

Some Obstacles to Board Evaluation

My experience indicates that very few boards of directors engage in regular and systematic evaluation of their own work. There are several obstacles to board evaluation which must be overcome. Following are some of the major ones: [1]

- **A perception on the part of some that it is unfair to subject the efforts of volunteers to critical appraisal.** Thoughtful board members, however, recognize that the responsibilities of boards are awesome and that evaluation must be conducted in order to update and improve board performance and practice.

- **Boards are very busy and many feel that they do not have the time for evaluation.** This obstacle is an easy way to avoid appraisal. The fact is that evaluation can be done without large time investments, as this chapter will demonstrate.

- **Critical inquiry and evaluation have a negative connotation for many people.** The focus of board evaluation, as many see it, is exclusively on deficiencies. They fail to see the positive contributions of reinforcement and improvement that evaluation and careful study make.

- **A view that the available instruments and methods for board evaluation are very imprecise.** Undoubtedly, an evaluation of any human endeavor is not as precise as some would prefer, but that should not be a deterrent to action. Indeed, subjective judgments have to be made even in those fields where the most precise tools are available.

160

Board Responsibility for Evaluation

The board of directors has multiple responsibilities for evaluation. As previously discussed, the board is responsible for evaluating the performance of the chief executive officer. Assistance for fulfilling this responsibility is available in Chapter 2. In addition, the board is responsible for monitoring achievement of the organization's goals and objectives and evaluating the effectiveness of the organization's programs and services. Assistance in accomplishing this broad-based responsibility for evaluation is amply available in the literature of planning and management.[2,3] There is considerably less assistance available in the literature, however, for evaluating the board itself; hence the focus of this chapter.

The responsibility for giving leadership to board evaluation necessarily rests with the board chair and the chief executive. This does not mean that these two must give personal and direct leadership to evaluation, but rather that they are responsible for ensuring that evaluation is satisfactorily accomplished. A special evaluation task force can be appointed or the assignment can be given to an existing committee or to an individual.

Evaluation of the board does not have to be complex and time consuming. In my judgment, board evaluation should be kept as simple and straightforward as possible. Although there may be infrequent occasions when an outside evaluation is necessary, in the vast majority of cases a board self-evaluation will more than suffice. It is suggested that boards briefly evaluate their functioning once or twice during the year and evaluate themselves much more extensively at the end of each year. In all cases board members should be involved in generating data that are fed back to the total board and used to derive action suggestions for self correction and improvement. Techniques for performing these kinds of evaluations, both during the year and on an annual basis, are delineated in the following sections.

161

During the Year
Evaluation Techniques

The following three techniques are designed to be conducted in brief periods of time as a part of regular board meetings during the year.[4]

● **Productivity Observer**—This technique involves appointing a member of the board to be an observer of the group's process. Generally, the productivity observer should be a person who is: 1) sensitive and objective in noting aspects of board functioning which can be improved; 2) well accepted and respected by the board; 3) able to verbalize observations to the board in a simple and objective manner without creating defensiveness or confusion. The productivity observer's job is to make observations and to start the ball of evaluation discussion rolling, rather than to hand down pronouncements that attempt to prove the observer's superiority. In performing the job, it is helpful for a productivity observer to use a *Productivity Observer Sheet* such as shown in Exhibit I.

● **Process Stops**—This technique involves conducting a ten to fifteen minute evaluation session. The session can be started by the board productivity observer's reporting the issues of his/her observations. If the observer technique is not used, process stops can simply be an evaluation discussion, with an appointed discussion leader asking such questions as: "How do you feel about our productivity and participation in this and recent board meetings?" "What have been the most productive parts of our meetings?" "Least productive?" "What hunches or ideas do you have that might help us improve the way we are working and make us more productive?"

Another way that I like to use this technique is to print the above kinds of questions along with specific directions for use and place these in a sealed envelope with instructions for each table group or sub-group of the board (about seven members). At a given time the person

162

Exhibit I

PRODUCTIVITY OBSERVER SHEET: BOARD OF DIRECTORS

Instructions:

Place a ✓ by the phrase that describes what you observe.

Place a X where the opposite of the phrase would describe what you observe.

____ 1. Members are clear on role and functions of board (i.e., distinguish clearly between board policy functions and staff management functions).

____ 2. Board has a real sense of responsibility for getting the job done.

____ 3. Board's work is related to the organization's goals and objectives.

____ 4. Continuity in board's work is evident; they build on previous work in efficient ways.

____ 5. Climate is one of mutual trust and openness. Atmosphere is friendly and relaxed.

____ 6. Creativity and individuality of board members are encouraged and respected.

____ 7. Leadership is shared among board members.

____ 8. Staff preparation is lacking. Board caught without adequate information, facts and documentation.

____ 9. Agenda items represent important issues that merit consideration of the board.

____ 10. Committees and task forces provide input and recommendations for board consideration.

____ 11. Decision making is superficial. The board is a "rubber stamp."

____ 12. Board stays on target with little topic jumping or going off on tangents.

____ 13. Silent members are bid into the discussions and deliberations.

____ 14. Members listen to each other and try hard to understand one another's ideas and suggestions.

____ 15. Members openly express feelings (i.e., irritation, anger, frustration, warmth, affection, excitement, boredom, etc.).

What did you think about the meeting?

1.	2.	3.	4.	5.	6.	7.

A Waste of Time   *Much Was Accomplished*

Exhibit I (*Cont'd*)

What were the strong points or most productive elements of the meeting?

What were the weak points or dysfunctional elements of the meeting?

What suggestions or ideas do you have for increasing the future effectiveness of board meetings?

Other comments?

nearest the envelope is asked to open the envelope and to follow the directions contained inside. I like to begin the written instructions with "CONGRATULATIONS! You have been specially selected to be our discussion leader."

Regardless of which adaptation of the process stop technique that is used, it is very important for the board to obtain consensus on what it is going to do to improve its methods of work and productivity.

● **Post Meeting Reactions**—Exhibit II is a post meeting reaction form that is designed for completion during the last five minutes of a board meeting. All forms should be collected immediately prior to adjournment and tabulated for report back at the next meeting of the board. At the next meeting the summary report should be followed by group discussion and consensus on what will be done to improve the work methods and productivity of the board.

Annual Evaluation Techniques

It is suggested that a more comprehensive evaluation of the board be conducted once each year. Exhibit III is an example of an evaluation instrument that focuses on the *process* elements of board functioning. Exhibit IV is an evaluation instrument based on *standards* for board functioning developed by the Public Management Institute of San Francisco.[5] It is suggested that the instruments or adaptations of them be used on alternate years. The instruments are both designed to be administered either prior to or in conjunction with the evaluation of the chief executive officer at the end of the organization's fiscal year. The instruments can be completed by members at the end of one board meeting and the summary of responses reported back at the next meeting. For the summary, Exhibit III is designed for computation of a mean (average) score for each item and Exhibit IV is designed for a

Exhibit II

POST MEETING REACTION FORM: BOARD MEMBERS

What did you think about the meeting? Please be frank. Your comments will be used to improve future meetings of the board.

1. How did you feel about the meeting generally?   (Check one)

    ☐   ☐   ☐   ☐   ☐
    Poor   *So-So*   *Average*   *Good*   *Tops*

2. What did you like *best* about the meeting?

3. What did you like *least* about the meeting?

4. What improvements would you suggest for making our next meeting better?

5. Please rate the following aspects of the meeting:

	Poor	*So-So*	*Average*	*Good*	*Tops*
YOUR INTEREST					
YOUR ENJOYMENT					
WORTH OF MEEETING					
WAY IT WAS CONDUCTED					
PARTICIPATION					

6. Other comments?

Exhibit III

BOARD OF DIRECTORS' EVALUATION

Name of Organization: _____

Your Name (optional): _____ Date: _____

Instructions: This document is designed to obtain <u>your</u> evaluation of the effectiveness of <u>your</u> organization's board of directors. Circle the number on the rating scale that corresponds to your evaluation of the board in each of the following categories. On item #1, for example, if you feel that clarity of role and function is lacking in the board, circle "1"; if you feel that clarity of role and function is somewhere in between, circle an appropriate number on the scale.

1. *Clarity of role and function* is lacking. We are fuzzy about what we are supposed to be doing.	1 2 3 4 5 6 7	*Clarity of role and function* is present. We distinguish clearly between policy determination and management functions. We know what we are about.
2. *Leadership* is dominated by one or a few persons and other resources within the board are never used.	1 2 3 4 5 6 7	*Leadership* is shared among members according to abilities and insights. Every member's resources are used.
3. *Important issues* are not dealt with but "swept under the rug" or dealt with outside of the board.	1 2 3 4 5 6 7	*Important issues* are consistently on the agenda for open consideration, debate and decision.
4. *Preparation* is lacking. We are consistently caught off guard without adequate information, facts and documentation.	1 2 3 4 5 6 7	*Preparation* is outstanding. Committees and staff do excellent preliminary work. Members are well informed and understand the pros and cons of all decisions.
5. *Communication of ideas* is poor. We do not really listen. Ideas are ignored.	1 2 3 4 5 6 7	*Communication of ideas* is good. We listen and try hard to understand one another's ideas. Ideas are well presented and acknowledged.
6. *Responsible participation* is lacking. We reflect our own biases. We "grind our own axes" and watch from "outside."	1 2 3 4 5 6 7	*Responsible participation* is present. We are sensitive to the need to reflect on what is best for our organization and the entire community. Everyone is "on the inside" participating.

Exhibit III (*Cont'd*)

7. *Acceptance of persons* is missing. Persons are rejected or ignored.

1 2 3 4 5 6 7

Acceptance of persons is an active part of our give-and-take. We recognize and respect the uniqueness of each person.

8. *Freedom of persons* is stifled. Conformity is explicitly or implicitly fostered. Persons do not feel free to express their individuality. They are manipulated.

1 2 3 4 5 6 7

Freedom of persons is enhanced and encouraged. The creativity and individuality of persons is respected.

9. *Climate of relationship* is one of hostility, suspicion, indulgent politeness, fear, anxiety or superficiality.

1 2 3 4 5 6 7

Climate of relationship is one of mutual trust and genuiness. The atmosphere is friendly and relaxed.

10. *Decision making* is superficial. We are really a "rubber stamp" for those on the "inside." Decisions are crammed down our throats.

1 2 3 4 5 6 7

Decision making is participative. All data are available and all opinions aired, with resultant "ownership" of decisions that are made.

11. *Action agreements* are not reached. We never set target dates or plan for follow-through.

1 2 3 4 5 6 7

Action agreements are reached. We agree on next steps to be taken and set target dates for review.

12. *Continuity* is lacking. At each meeting we seem to "start from scratch."

1 2 3 4 5 6 7

Continuity is present. We build on previous work in an efficient way.

13. *Productivity* is low. We are proud, fat and happy—just coasting along. Our meetings are a waste of time and money.

1 2 3 4 5 6 7

Productivity is high. We are digging hard and earnestly at work on important tasks. We create and achieve at each meeting.

Finally . . .

Based on the above evaluation, what suggestions or ideas do you have for increasing the effectiveness of your organization's board? (NOTE: Give particular attention to ways of strengthening the items which you rated 4 or below.)

Exhibit IV

EVALUATE YOUR BOARD OF DIRECTORS

ACTIVITY	Check One		SUGGESTIONS FOR IMPROVEMENT
	YES	NO	
1. Board operates under a clear and up-to-date set of by-laws with which all members are familiar.			
2. Board has an elected executive committee which reports fully to the board on all actions taken.			
3. Board has standing committees which meet regularly and report back.			
4. Eighty percent of board members attend meetings.			
5. Every board member serves on at least one committee.			
6. Board has diversity of experience, skills, ethnic, racial, gender and age groups.			
7. Nominating committee uses established criteria to recruit board members based on the needs of the board.			
8. Newly elected board members are fully oriented to what is expected.			
9. Board includes in each meeting some educational or interpretation time.			
10. Board members are elected for a specific term.			
11. Board has completed both long range and short-term planning.			
12. Board meets at least 9 times yearly.			

Exhibit IV (*Cont'd*)

ACTIVITY	Check One		SUGGESTIONS FOR IMPROVEMENT
	YES	NO	
13. Board receives their agenda in advance.			
14. Staff participates in committee and board meetings as appropriate.			
15. There is an orderly procedure for decision making at board meetings.			
16. Board conducts an annual review of its work and operating procedures.			
17. Board reviews, approves and monitors the budget. Members understand the reports.			
18. Board has formal executive appraisal method.			
19. There is a trustful and harmonious relationship between board and staff.			
20. Board members receive all appropriate information (positive and negative) necessary to make policy decisions.			
21. Board discussions are free with full participation and respect for divergent opinions.			
22. All board members provide some leadership to the annual campaign.			
23. All board members contribute annually to the fund raising campaign.			
24. Board works with other organizations in the community and is familiar with their goals and activities.			

NAME: (optional) _____ ORGANIZATION: _____ DATE: _____

Source of Standards: Public Management Institute

frequency count (yes or no) for each item. "Suggestions for Improvement" on both instruments should be content analyzed and included as a part of the summary report. Following the summary report and questions of clarification, consensus should be obtained through group discussion on what the board intends to do to improve either its work processes or its performance in meeting desired standards.

Finally . . .

It is certainly possible for a board to become so involved in carrying out its many responsibilities that it neglects the task of evaluating itself. Such an oversight makes the entire organization subject to the creeping malaise of mediocrity because of the pervasive impact of the board on qualitative functioning. Systematic evaluation can be extremely helpful without being overly time consuming. Without evaluation, board development has little or no focus. With evaluation, board development becomes a vigorous and spirited pursuit of individual and collective excellence.

NOTES: Chapter 11

1. *Citizen Board Development Program.* Big Brothers/Big Sisters of America, 1984, pp. 40–41.

2. Hardy, James M. *Managing for Impact in Nonprofit Organizations.* Essex Press, 1984, pp. 177–204.

3. O'Connell, Brian. *Evaluating Results.* Independent Sector, 1988, pp. 15–24.

4. Hardy, James M. *Corporate Planning for Nonprofit Organizations.* Association Press, 1972, pp. 18–22.

5. Public Management Institute exhibited in *Successful Board Leadership.* Management Resource Center YMCA's of Southern California, 1984, pp. 42–43.

Afterword:
Looking Ahead

Introduction

The major thesis of this book is that the leaders of effective nonprofit organizations in the late 20th century must be proactive in developing their organization's board of directors. I have written the book to help equip and enable or empower, if you will, the organization's leadership to accomplish this vital task.

As noted in the text, all of the concepts, processes and techniques described in this book have been tested in a variety of nonprofit organizations of different sizes. All of these work and contribute to effective board functioning. But will these concepts, processes and techniques be relevant and helpful in the future? Even more importantly, will boards of directors be as pivotal in the future for organizational effectiveness as they currently are? Obviously, no one can answer these questions with certainty, but the questions are important and merit consideration. The purpose of this afterword is to take a brief look at the future in order to provide the reader a basis for reflecting on the future relevancy of the concepts, processes and techniques in this book and the future importance of boards of directors. More specifically, in the afterword I will highlight some future trends affecting nonprofit organizations and hazard a guess about the future importance of boards. Finally, I will suggest some specific ways for making board development continuous; ways that can result in constant improvement and relevancy as we move toward the 21st century and beyond.

172

Some Future Trends

Following are a limited number of trends from a variety of studies of the future and my own environmental scanning efforts regarding nonprofit organizations.[1] These are certainly not inclusive; that is not the intent. Rather, I have been highly selective of trends which hope-fully will assist the reader in discerning the shape of the future within which nonprofit organizations will function.

- Competition for donors and funds will intensify in the future due primarily to a proliferation of active nonprofit organi-zations and Federal budget cuts. Although the overall eco-nomic situation is expected to be generally good, there will be cyclic ups and downs. These forces, combined with the loss of fund raising capability on the part of many nonprofits, will result in a long-term money crunch.

- More and more nonprofits will search for cooperative ap-proaches to solving problems, due in part to the competition for funds. Corporations, entrepreneurs, investors and the pub-lic sector will be joining nonprofit organizations in these co-operative endeavors.

- For-profit entrepreneurs will increasingly provide services that are the same as or similar to those traditionally provided by nonprofits—such as day care, health care, counseling, sub-stance abuse treatment and fitness. Conflicts with nonprofits will multiply. Small business entrepreneurs will bring pres-sure to have non-profit organizations prohibited from engag-ing in profit-making activities because of an alleged unfair advantage of tax exemption and other favored circumstances enjoyed by nonprofits. Government agencies will increase their scrutiny of business operations of nonprofits with a view toward identifying "unrelated business income" and/or plac-ing nonprofits on the tax rolls.

173

- Pressure will increase from several sources for nonprofits to justify themselves, improve their accountability and provide measures of performance and effectiveness. A growing importance will be attached to adherence to mission and charitable purpose, formulation of explicit goals and objectives, and to the creation of organizational focus in an era of change.

- Due to the rising tide of litigation, nonprofits will continue to encounter dramatically increased insurance premiums, reduced coverage and, in some cases, loss of coverage entirely. Activities and services, ranging from high school sports to day care, will be drastically affected.

- Government regulation of nonprofit organizations will increase in the future. Most nonprofits will find compliance to be burdensome and costly.

- Nonprofit organizations and businesses will establish closer working relationships. Businesses will increasingly provide volunteers who have technical specialties (i.e., management, research, accounting, law, etc.).

- Effective nonprofit organizations in the future will give major attention to the development of all their human resources— both staff and volunteers.

- Boards of directors will be more active, involved and aware of their legal responsibilities and fiduciary duties in the future. This trend derives from a number of related trends that affect nonprofit organizations: decreased government funding; increased social need; and close scrutiny of the press, the legal profession and the general public. These trends, combined with others emerging in the future, will essentially force nonprofit boards to be better informed, more active and involved.

Importance of Boards
in the Future

My crystal ball is no clearer than any others, but I have no hesitancy in emphatically suggesting that boards of directors will be even more necessary for effective organizational functioning in the future than they are at the present. Because boards are exceedingly important today, that's saying a lot. However, if the shape of the future environment for nonprofits is anything like that described previously, it seems apparent that dynamic boards will be absolutely critical to effective organizational functioning. The environment of the future will simply not tolerate uninformed boards that perfunctorily rubber-stamp staff decisions or attempt to manage rather than to govern.

In the future, boards will give much more attention to setting the organization's direction—mission, goals and objectives; establishing policies to guide the organization; ensuring adequate financing and fiscal responsibility; monitoring achievement; and providing credibility and enthusiastic endorsement of the organization in the community. For effective nonprofit organizations of the future this will require placing a premium on the recruitment and development of board members who are capable of intelligent, informed inquiry that leads to enlightened and significant action.

Keeping Relevant in the Future

It must be obvious at this point that board development, by its very nature, is continuous, rather than being a one-time or limited activity. In order to be effective, board development must result in constant improvement. It's what the Japanese call KAIZEN and it's an absolute requirement for keeping relevant in the future. But how do leaders ensure that board development results in constant board improvement? There are many ways, but certainly a critical one is through on-going assessment of board development itself. Appendix A is a comprehensive board development assessment instrument that is designed to assist an organization in constantly renewing its board development program and keeping it current and relevant. Appendix B is an assessment response grid to be completed by each respondent and Appendix C is a tabulation sheet that, when completed, indicates the dimensions of board development of greatest need to the organization.

It is suggested that the Board Development Assessment be completed each year by the entire board of directors or by members of the board development committee. Upon identification of the dimensions of greatest need, the board development committee can utilize Appendix D which provides a key for obtaining assistance on each dimension of board development. The references in Appendix D are located in either this book or in *Managing for Impact in Nonprofit Organizations*.[2] By making an annual assessment of board development and using Appendix D, a continuous board development program can be constructed that results in constant improvement and renewal.

In Conclusion . . .

Over the years it has been my great privilege to have worked with and served on literally hundreds of boards of nonprofit organizations. In sum, these experiences have been very *satisfying, pleasurable* and *learningful* for me. I covet the same for each person who serves as a member of a nonprofit board of directors.

I think the experience of serving on a nonprofit board should be *satisfying* in terms of the ultimate contributions that are made to and with people. I think the experience should be *pleasurable* in terms of the enjoyment and sheer fun of serving with people of like conviction, good will and delightful humor. Lastly, I think the experience should be *learningful* in terms of how one learns and grows through the broadening and insightful opportunities and meaningful relationships provided by board service.

For an organization to be a dynamic, vital and effective force in society requires, and will undoubtedly continue to require, men and women who are members of its board to be persons of caliber and high calling. They must be informed about the organization. They must establish challenging and attainable directions, imaginative strategies and policies which effectively guide the organization's work. They must develop a productive partnership with staff and conduct themselves, not as operating managers, but as men and women charged with the accountability of preserving and enhancing the character, growth and influence of the organization in the lives of people and in the community. Then, through its vision, actions, dedication to task and commitment to purpose, the organization's board of directors will truly serve as trustee and steward of the future.

NOTES: *Afterword*

1. Hardy, James M. *Moving Toward the 21st Century.* JMH Associates, 1988, pp. 16–21.
2. Hardy, James M. *Managing for Impact in Nonprofit Organizations.* Essex Press, 1984.

177

Part Three

Appendix and Bibliography

Appendix A

Board Development Assessment

Instructions:

1. Use the "Assessment Response Grid" for recording your responses to the seventy statements listed below and on the following pages. Numbers in each square of the grid correspond to the numbers of the statements. If, in your opinion, a statement is *generally* true about your organization's board of directors, mark the appropriate square with an "X." If you think a statement is *not generally* true, leave the square blank.

2. Work through the statements in numerical order.

3. Do not spend a lot of time thinking about each statement. Your first impression is probably your best response.

4. Be honest and candid in your responses. Anything less will not be helpful to your organization.

STATEMENTS:

1. Board member attendance and participation are below acceptable levels.

2. There is no specific plan and corresponding methods for recruiting new board members.

3. New board members do not receive a formal orientation to the organization and to their board responsibilities.

4. The organization's by-laws are not complete, clear and up-to-date concerning the organization's purpose, board structure and functioning.

5. The board has too many standing committees and too few short-term ad hoc groups.

6. Board meetings are often a waste of time.

181

7. Board discussions tend to be constrained, guarded and inhibited. There is little or no respect for divergent opinion.

8. The board has no orderly process for decision making.

9. There is little openness, trust and mutual respect between the board and staff.

10. The board makes no formal annual appraisal of the performance of the chief executive officer.

11. The board has no on-going process for examining significant internal and external trends affecting the organization.

12. Board appraisal and periodic reviews of the budget are perfunctory and ineffective.

13. Not all board members make an annual financial contribution to the organization.

14. Media news releases (radio, TV, newspapers, etc.) very seldom spotlight the contributions of board members.

15. Board membership is not balanced and as diverse as it should be (experience, skill, race, gender, age, etc.).

16. There is no board member job description or clearly written statement outlining the duties and responsibilities of board members.

17. There is no identification of board member training needs and program of board member training that is carried out throughout the year.

18. Board tenure is unlimited. There is no periodic rotation of board members.

19. Committee responsibilities and assignments are not in writing and supplied to all members.

20. Board meetings seldom start and end on time.

21. Board leadership is highly centralized and restricted to one or a few persons.

22. Board members do not receive all information (positive and negative) necessary to make appropriate decisions.

23. Board members are frequently involved in operational and administrative matters which should be the responsibility of staff.

24. Generally, the board functions without regard to what other community organizations are doing. There is little or no effort placed on inter-agency collaboration.

25. The board is not involved in formulating and approving the organization's long range goals.

26. Financial reports are not understood by most board members.

27. The board does not have a resource development plan which ensures that the organization has adequate resources to achieve its goals and objectives.

28. There is little or no provision or practice to promote effective board members to higher positions of responsibility and authority.

29. Selection of new board members is not determined by needed or desired characteristics.

30. Prospective board members are rarely, if ever, recruited on a face-to-face basis by a team of the prospect's peers.

31. Live participant reports and program demonstrations for educational purposes are not on the agenda of board meetings.

32. The board meets less than six times per year.

33. Active committees are rare. The entire board does almost all of the work.

34. Routine matters which require action but little discussion are not handled with dispatch and efficiency in board meetings.

35. Communication in the board is poor. Members do not really listen to each other.

36. Important issues are not dealt with by the board—they are either ignored or dealt with outside of the board.

37. The roles, responsibilities and relationships of board members and staff are not clearly delineated.

38. Board members do not usually function as active vocal proponents of the organization but rather view this mainly as a staff function.

39. The board does not systematically review the organization's performance in relationship to its mission, goals and objectives.

40. The board takes little or no responsibility for ensuring that the organization maintains a fiscally solvent financial condition.

41. Committees are not active in the design and implementation of a comprehensive financial development program.

42. No consideration is generally given to individual recognition needs of board members.

43. The board has more "dead wood" on it—members who do not actively contribute—than it should have.

44. Responsibilities and time demands of effective board service are frequently understated when persons are recruited for board membership.

45. There is no up-to-date *Board Member's Manual* which is given to all members.

46. Board members do not understand their personal liabilities and legal responsibilities.

47. Attendance at committee meetings is generally poor and real contributions are spotty.

48. The majority of board meeting time is devoted to listening to reports rather than to policy determination, review of plans and evaluation of the work of the organization.

49. The board is inefficient—it seldom builds on previous work.

50. The board is a rubber stamp for staff and for those on the "inside." There is very little real participation in decision making.

51. In many instances, staff are solely involved in determining organizational policy which should be determined by the board.

52. The board does not conduct an annual review of its own work and operating procedures.

53. The board does not approve and is not generally aware of the organization's short-term (one year) objectives.

54. A financial audit of the organization is not conducted on a regular and timely basis.

55. Many board members do not consider fund raising to be a responsibility of the board of directors.

56. Board member accomplishments are not regularly highlighted in the organization's newsletter or other publications.

57. The board of directors is weak. It is not composed of the kinds of people needed to move the organization ahead.

58. No special training is provided for board recruiters. They just "do what comes naturally."

59. Generally, board members do not participate in training programs outside of the local organization.

60. The size of the board is inappropriate (i.e., too large or too small).

61. The board seldom makes use of ad hoc groups or temporary task forces.

62. The board's agenda and preparatory materials are not sent out routinely prior to all board meetings.

63. Member resources are not consistently well used in the work of the board.

64. The board almost always uses Robert's Rules of Order in making decisions.

65. The relationship between the board chairperson and the chief executive officer tends to be formal, strained and closed.

66. The board does not assume sole responsibility for determining policy.

67. The budgeting process is unrelated to the organization's long-term goals and short-term objectives.

68. There is no budget and finance committee of the board (or similar group) that closely monitors and reviews all fiscal operations.

69. The board neither gives leadership to nor does it participate in the organization's fund raising efforts.

70. Board members are seldom, if ever, recognized and appreciated for their contributions and accomplishments.

Appendix B

Assessment Response Grid

- Follow the instructions given at the beginning of the "Board Development Assessment" instrument.

- In the grid below are seventy squares; each one numbered to correspond to a statement in the "Board Development Assessment" instrument. Mark an "X" through the square if you think a statement about your organization is *generally* true. If you think a statement is not generally true, leave the square blank.

- Fill in the top line that has numbers first, working from left to right; then fill in the next line, etc. Be careful not to miss a statement. Disregard the letters (A through N) that mark each column.

A	B	C	D	E	F	G	H	I	J	K	L	M	N
1.	2.	3.	4.	5.	6.	7.	8.	9.	10.	11.	12.	13.	14.
15.	16.	17.	18.	19.	20.	21.	22.	23.	24.	25.	26.	27.	28.
29.	30.	31.	32.	33.	34.	35.	36.	37.	38.	39.	40.	41.	42.
43.	44.	45.	46.	47.	48.	49.	50.	51.	52.	53.	54.	55.	56.
57.	58.	59.	60.	61.	62.	63.	64.	65.	66.	67.	68.	69.	70.

TOTALS

- When you have completed all seventy statements, count the number of "X's" in each vertical column (A through N) and write the total in the appropriate square at the bottom of the grid.

- Thanks for your assistance. Later you will receive an interpretation of the results.

YOUR NAME (Optional): _____

POSITION IN ORGANIZATION: _____

* Response Grid adapted from: Dave Francis and Mike Woodcock. *People at Work*. University Associates, 1975, p. 32.

Appendix C

Tabulation Sheet
ASSESSMENT RESPONSE GRID

1.	2.	3.	4.	5.
GRID COLUMN	TOTALS FROM GRID	TOTAL X's	DIMENSIONS OF BOARD DEVELOPMENT	RANK PRIORITY OF NEED
A			COMPOSITION	
B			RECRUITMENT	
C			ORIENTATION & TRAINING	
D			STRUCTURE	
E			COMMITTEES	
F			MEETINGS	
G			WORK CLIMATE	
H			DECISION MAKING	
I			BOARD/STAFF RELATIONSHIPS	
J			BOARD FUNCTIONING	
K			PLANNING	
L			FISCAL RESPONSIBILITIES	
M			FINANCIAL DEVELOPMENT	
N			RECOGNITION	

Instructions:

- Transfer the totals from the "Assessment Response Grid" to column 2 above for each of the column letters (A through N).

- Add the numbers in column 2 above and place the total in column 3 ("Total X's").

- Column 4 above indicates the dimensions of board development being assessed. The totals in column 3 suggest the need.

- In column 5, rank the dimensions according to the totals in column 3 (i.e., dimension with highest total in column 3 is ranked "1" in column 5; second highest total is ranked "2," etc.). This suggests the dimensions of greatest need for your organization.

Note: This assessment is designed to assist organizations in determining the dimensions of board development that need strengthening. The specifics within each dimension can be identified by checking the frequency of each of the seventy statements on the "Assessment Response Grid." The dimensions of greatest need noted above in column 5 and the highest frequency counts of individual statements provide an excellent basis for constructing a comprehensive board development program for the organization.

187

Appendix D

BOARD DEVELOPMENT KEY:
FROM ASSESSMENT TO ASSISTANCE

* Pages in *Developing Dynamic Boards*. Essex Press, 1990.
** Pages in *Managing for Impact in Nonprofit Organizations*. Essex Press, 1984.

DIMENSIONS OF BOARD DEVELOPMENT	REFERENCES FOR ASSISTANCE
A. Composition	*Pp.49–72
B. Recruitment	*Pp. 25–27; 72–78
C. Orientation and Training	*Pp. 79–93
D. Structure	*Pp. 23–25; 94–103
E. Committees	*Pp. 97–107
F. Meetings	*Pp. 108–119
G. Work Climate	*Pp. 113–118; 120–124
H. Decision Making	*Pp. 120–134
I. Board/Staff Relationships	*Pp. 30–47
J. Board Functioning	*Pp. 9–23; 141–153
K. Planning	*Pp. 10, 19–20
	**Pp. 3–205
L. Fiscal Responsibilities	*Pp. 18–19
	**Pp. 159–174
M. Financial Development	*Pp. 17–18
	**Pp. 103–122
N. Recognition	*Pp. 135–140

188

Bibliography

1. Abbott, Charles C. *Governance—A Guide for Trustees and Directors.* The Cheswick Center, 1979.

2. Axelrod, Nancy R. *The Chief Executive's Role in Developing the Nonprofit Board.* National Center for Nonprofit Boards, 1988.

3. Bacon, Jeremy. "Corporate Directorship Practices." Quoted in *Harvard Business Review,* May–June, 1982.

4. Barbeito, Carol L. *Doing Good Can Mean Doing Well.* Technical Assistance Center, 1985.

5. Behn, Robert D. and James W. Vaupel. *Quick Analysis for Busy Decision Makers.* Basic Books, Inc., 1982.

6. Bradford, Leland P. *Making Meetings Work.* University Associates, 1976.

7. Chait, Richard P. and Barbara E. Taylor. "Charting the Territory of Nonprofit Boards." *Harvard Business Review,* January–February, 1989.

8. *Citizen Board Development.* Big Brothers/Big Sisters of America, 1984.

9. Conrad, W. R., Jr. and W. E. Glenn. *The Effective Voluntary Board of Directors.* Swallow Press, 1983.

10. Dayton, Kenneth W. *Governance Is Governance.* Independent Sector, 1987.

11. Didactic Systems, Inc. *The Citizen Board in Voluntary Agencies.* United Way of America, 1979.

12. Dolan, Robert. *The Leadership Development Process.* 4-H Volunteer-Staff Development, Undated.

13. Drucker, Peter F. "What Business Can Learn from Nonprofits." *Harvard Business Review,* July–August, 1989.

189

14. Eberhardt, Louise. "Holding Productive and Satisfying Board Meetings." *The Nonprofit Board Book.* Independent Community Consultants, 1985.

15. Educational Services Unit. *Volunteer Resource Book.* Girl Scouts of the U.S.A., 1982.

16. Fenn, Dan H., Jr. "Executives As Community Volunteers." *Harvard Business Review,* March–April, 1971.

17. Forbess-Greene, Sue. *The Encyclopedia of Icebreakers.* Applied Skills Press, 1980.

18. *Formal Education of Nonprofit Organization Leaders/Managers.* Independent Sector, 1988.

19. Fram, Eugene H. "Nonprofit Boards: They're Going Corporate." *Board Leadership and Governance.* The Society for Nonprofit Organizations, 1989.

20. Francis, Dave and Mike Woodcock. *People at Work.* University Associates, 1975.

21. Gardner, John W. "The Independent Sector." *America's Voluntary Spirit,* Brian O'Connell. The Foundation Center, 1983.

22. Gates, Virginia E., editor. *Helping Hands.* YMCA of Metropolitan Chicago, 1979.

23. Hall, Jay. *Ponderables.* Teleometrics International, 1982.

24. Hall, Jay. *Toward Group Effectiveness.* Teleometrics International, 1971.

25. Hardy, James M. *Moving Toward the 21st Century.* JMH Associates, 1988.

26. Hardy, James M. *Corporate Board Orientation: A Ministry of Service.* Volunteers of America, 1986.

27. Hardy, James M. *Managing for Impact in Nonprofit Organizations: Corporate Planning Techniques and Applications.* Essex Press, 1984.

28. Hardy, James M. *Assessing and Strengthening the YMCA's Board of Directors.* YMCA of USA South Field Office, 1981.

29. Hardy, James M. *Managing Individual Development.* JMH Associates, 1980.

30. Hardy, James M. *The Corporate Board in the YMCA.* YMCA of USA, 1980.

31. Hardy, James M. *A YMCA Tool Kit: Complete Orientation Program for YMCA Board Members.* YMCA of USA, 1980.

32. Hardy, James M. *Corporate Planning for Nonprofit Organizations.* Association Press, 1972.

33. Hodgetts, R. M. and M. S. Wortman, Jr. "Decisions at Different Policy Levels" in "Charting the Territory of Nonprofit Boards" by Richard P. Chait and Barbara E. Taylor. *Harvard Business Review,* January–February, 1989.

34. Houle, Cyril. *The Effective Board.* Association Press, 1960.

35. Houle, Cyril. *Governing Boards.* Jossey-Bass Publishers, 1989.

36. Howe, Fisher. *Fund Raising and the Nonprofit Board Member.* National Center for Nonprofit Boards, 1988.

37. Kuenzli, Gary. *Successful Board Leadership.* Management Resource Center, YMCA's of Southern California, 1984.

38. Kurtz, Daniel L. *Board Liability.* Moyer Bell Limited, 1988.

39. Lippincott, E. and E. Aannestad. "Management of Voluntary Welfare Agencies." *Harvard Business Review,* Vol. 46, No. 6, 1964.

40. Lowry, Sheldon G. and John S. Holik. *A New Look at Parliamentary Procedure.* North Central Regional Extension Publications, 1985.

41. *Management Guide for Arkansas Nonprofit Organizations.* Arkansas Department of Human Services, 1987.

42. Manswer, Gordon and Rosemary Higgins Cass. *Voluntarism at the Crossroads.* Family Service Association of America, 1976.

191

43. Marrow, A. J., D. G. Bower and S. E. Seashore. *Management by Participation.* Harper and Row, 1967.

44. Middleton, Melissa. "Nonprofit Boards of Directors: Beyond the Governance Function." *The Nonprofit Sector* edited by Walter W. Powell. Yale University Press, 1987.

45. Mill, Cyril R. *Activities for Trainers.* University Associates, 1980.

46. Moore, Carl M. *Group Techniques for Idea Building.* Sage Publications, 1987.

47. Morgan, Mark. "Does Your Board Include Bankers? Here's How to Find Local Leaders." *Perspective Magazine,* May, 1989.

48. Munson, Mary K. *Educational Methods and Techniques.* University of Illinois 4-H Youth, 1987.

49. Munson, Mary K. *Creative Recognition Ideas.* University of Illinois 4-H Youth, 1987.

50. Nason, John W. *Presidential Assessment.* Association of Governing Boards of Universities and Colleges, 1984.

51. Nason, John W. *An Inquiry into Current Program Toward Strengthening the Performance of Board Members of Nonprofit Organizations.* Association of Governing Boards of Universities and Colleges, 1984.

52. Newby, Jack M., Jr. "How to Measure Your Board the Quantitative Way." *Perspective Magazine,* September, 1978.

53. Nutt, Paul C. *Making Tough Decisions.* Jossey-Bass Publishers, 1989.

54. O'Connell, Brian. *Nonprofit Management Series* (9 booklets). Independent Sector, 1988.

55. O'Connell, Brian. *The Board Member's Book.* The Foundation Center, 1985.

56. O'Connell, Brian. *America's Voluntary Spirit.* The Foundation Center, 1983.

57. O'Connell, Brian. *Effective Leadership in Voluntary Organizations.* Walker and Company, 1981.

58. Patton, Arch and John C. Baker. "Why Won't Directors Rock the Boat?" *Harvard Business Review*, November–December, 1987.

59. Poummit, Morris R. "Are Your Board Meetings Bored Meetings?" *Nonprofit World*, 1988.

60. Pruett, M. and D. Wells. *Reviewing and Appraising Performance in Girl Scouting*. Girl Scouts of the U.S.A., 1986.

61. Reno, Kyle. *Manual for Board Members of Not-For-Profit Organizations*. Technical Assistance Center, Denver, 1986.

62. Rudney, Gabriel. "The Scope and Dimensions of Nonprofit Activity." *The Nonprofit Sector* edited by Walter W. Powell, Yale University Press, 1987.

63. Schoderbek, Peter P. *The Board and Its Responsibilities*. United Way of America, 1983.

64. Sorenson, Roy. *The Art of Board Membership*. Association Press, 1953.

65. Stone, Byron and Carol North. *Risk Management and Insurance for Nonprofit Managers*. First Nonprofit Risk Pooling Trust, 1988.

66. Swanson, Andrew. *Building A Better Board*. The Taft Group, 1984.

67. *The Responsibilities of a Director of a New York, New Jersey or Connecticut Nonprofit Corporation*. The Volunteer Urban Consulting Group, 1978.

68. *The Responsibilities of a Nonprofit Organization's Volunteer Board*. Council of Better Business Bureaus, Inc., 1988.

69. Titmuss, Richard M. *The Gift Relationship: From Human Blood to Social Policy*. Pantheon Books, 1971.

70. Trecker, Harleigh B. *Citizen Boards at Work*. Association Press, 1970.

71. Tropman, John E. *Effective Meetings: Improving Group Decision-Making*. Sage Publications, 1980.

72. Ulvila, Jacob W. and Rex V. Brown. "Decision Analysis Comes of Age." *Harvard Business Review*, September–October, 1982.

73. Unterman, Israel and Richard H. Davis. "The Strategy Gap in Not-For-Profits." *Harvard Business Review,* May–June, 1982.

74. Vance, Stanley. *The Corporate Director,* quoted in *Perspective Magazine,* 1978.

75. Vineyard, Sue. *Beyond Banquets, Plaques and Pens: Creative Ways to Recognize Volunteers and Staff.* Heritage Arts, 1981.

76. Weber, Joseph. *Managing the Board of Directors.* The Greater New York Fund, 1975.

77. Weisbrod, Burton A. *The Nonprofit Economy.* Harvard University Press, 1989.